PEARL HARBOR

PEARL HARBOR

STEPHEN BADSEY

MALLARD PRESS

First published in the United States of America
in 1991
by The Mallard Press
Mallard Press and its accompanying design and
logo are trademarks of BDD Promotional Book
Company, Inc.

ISBN 0-7924-5640-8

Printed in Hong Kong

PAGE 1, LEFT TO RIGHT: The battleships
West Virginia, Tennessee, and *Arizona*
on fire during the Japanese attack on
Pearl Harbor.

PAGES 2-3: The USS *Arizona* sinking at
anchor in Battleship Row.

THESE PAGES: The USS *Nevada*
attempts to escape the Japanese
bombs.

CONTENTS

INTRODUCTION

FROM ABOUT 0740 hours to 1030 hours local time on Sunday 7 December 1941, the principal US Navy base in the Pacific Ocean, at Pearl Harbor on Oahu in the Hawaiian Islands, was attacked without warning by a force of some 353 aircraft launched by surprise from six aircraft carriers of the Japanese Imperial Navy, so bringing about a state of war between the United States and Japan which was to last until the unconditional surrender of the Japanese armed forces on 15 August 1945.

This much is fact. But almost with the sound of the departing Japanese aircraft legends began to cluster around the attack. After so many years, like the hull of an old warship, the Pearl Harbor story is so deeply encrusted with investigations, cover-ups, theories, opinions, concealments, attitudes, half-truths, myths, boasts and simple lies, that the answer to the most simple of questions about Pearl Harbor – *why* the Japanese attacked – is buried almost beyond reach forever.

Still, the story is worth telling, as simply and as clearly as possible. Even today, the aftermath of the war between the United States and Japan continues to shape the existence of the Pacific world and the relationships between the countries that border the world's largest ocean. Pearl Harbor was beyond doubt a great and daring feat of arms. But it is also far more than just a 'war story.' Even though most of those who took part are now dead, the story itself continues to live.

The explanation for the events of 1941 does not lie on the surface, but must be sought for deep in the past. The story is actually three stories, deeply intertwined, that must be told together to be properly understood. First is the story of the emergence of Japan, after centuries of deliberately hiding from the world, to become a modern industrial nation and the dominant power in the Far East by 1941. The speed of the Japanese achievement was, by any standards,

astonishing. But, like any rapid transformation, it created problems for Japan and other countries, which could finally be resolved only by war.

The second story tells of the emergence, just slightly ahead of Japan, of the United States as a major power on the Pacific rim. In a sense, early twentieth century Japan was almost an American creation, a Frankenstein's monster that finally turned on its creator. The motives of the United States in first becoming a Pacific power must be understood if the reason behind the Japanese attack on Pearl Harbor is to be explained.

The third story is the story of the Pacific itself, and of the mighty warships that represented Japanese and American power on that ocean. It is the story of the development of naval warfare leading to the creation of the great battle fleets, and to their eclipse by the aircraft carrier at Pearl Harbor. It is more than fitting that this story both begins and ends on board a ship.

BELOW LEFT: Pearl Harbor in 1941, looking south toward the entrance, showing Ford Island in the center of the harbor and Battleship Row anchorage on the left of the island.

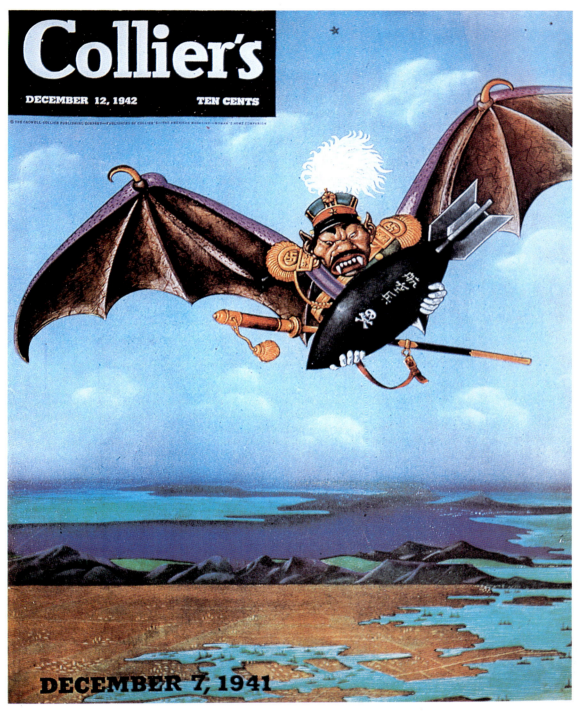

ABOVE RIGHT: The American view of Pearl Harbor as depicted in a magazine cover published five days after the attack.

RIGHT: President Franklin D. Roosevelt in 1941.

FAR RIGHT: The Japanese view of Pearl Harbor as shown in a magazine cover showing an Imperial Navy pilot as a hero with a Samurai sword.

CHAPTER ONE

MANIFEST DESTINY

THE ANCHOR on its chain slid into the depths of Edo Bay, and the great ship came to rest. It was 8 July 1853, one of those rare dates in history after which nothing could ever be the same again. The steamships USS *Susquehanna* and USS *Mississippi*, together with the sloops USS *Plymouth* and USS *Saratoga*, had brought Commodore Matthew Calbraith Perry of the US Navy to Japan with instructions from President Millard Fillmore to negotiate the opening up of a country that had been closed to foreigners for more than two centuries. A few of the children who watched Perry's arrival would still be alive when this intrusion by the United States into Japanese affairs was repaid at Pearl Harbor. Before then, much – not all of it predestined – was to happen.

Perry's ships were 'great' only to the Japanese. The *Susquehanna* and *Mississippi* were barque-rigged paddle frigates of 3220 tons displacement. The United States did not possess, and would not possess for more than 30 years, a single warship capable of fighting against the great navies of Europe. But in 1853 Japan had no navy at all. Since 1638 the Japanese had actively turned their backs on the outside world, and on the Industrial Revolution that had transformed Europe and America, including their military might. The first Europeans to arrive in Japan, Spanish and Portuguese traders and missionaries, had come in 1542. But about 50 years after their arrival a major civil war broke out in Japan, from which the Togugawa dynasty of *Shoguns* ('protectors') emerged supreme in 1603. The Japanese Emperor, who traced his ancestors back to 660 BC, continued to rule in name only from his capital of Kyoto, while actual political power lay in the Shogunate capital of Edo. Over the next 30 years decrees were passed expelling foreigners and denying all rights of entry to Japan. All overseas trade was forbidden, except on a small scale with Imperial China and with the Dutch through their tiny colony in Nagasaki Bay, and no vessel larger than a small fishing boat could be built. Any foreigner (*gaijin*, for which 'barbarian' is a polite translation) attempting to enter Japan was liable to imprisonment or worse. This included *gaijin* sailors who had the misfortune to be shipwrecked on Japanese shores.

Contact between Japan and the Western powers did not resume until the end of the eighteenth century. For about 50 years there were occasional Western embassies to Japan, always ignored by the Shogunate. The Japanese were afraid of direct contact with the West, particularly after the British, in the Opium War of 1842-3, forced the opening up of Imperial Chinese ports to Western trade and acquired Hong Kong as their own trading base. Japan was not anxious to risk the same fate by dealing with the barbarians.

This policy of *sakoku* ('closed country') succeeded until 1853 chiefly because Japan had very little that the foreigners actually wanted. Japan consists of four main islands plus more than 3000 islands and islets reaching from the Kurile Islands to Okinawa, the equivalent of the distance from Seattle almost to the southern end of the Gulf of California. But the actual land area of Japan is no more than 145,000 square miles, rather less than California itself. Most of the country is mountainous and volcanic, subject to earthquakes (this, together with the lack of natural resources, explained the Japanese custom of building houses of wood and paper) and only about 15 percent of the land could be used for agriculture. Into this rather small area were crammed, at the end of the nineteenth century, some 30 to 40 million people in a feudal society which stressed the unimportance of the individual, a rigid social hierarchy, and (not surprisingly) good manners and harmony from all. Japan could just about feed and clothe itself, being virtually self-sufficient in rice, soya, silk and cotton, but it had none of the resources of a modern industrial state. In particular, Japan had no oil, virtually no iron ore, and only limited reserves of coal.

What brought Commodore Perry to Edo Bay was the American emergence onto the Pacific, promoted by what a generation of American politicians called the 'Manifest Destiny' of the United States to expand westward. In 1844 Oregon petitioned the US Congress for the status of a territory, and two years later its northern boundary was agreed with the British. The Republic of Texas was annexed by the United States in 1845, and the Mexican War of 1846-8 added California (where gold was discovered a year later, prompting the '49 Gold Rush). The western frontier of the United States, virtually static since the Louisiana Purchase of 1803, moved a thousand miles to the Pacific in four years. In 1867 the Russian Empire sold to the Americans its claim to the territory of Alaska, giving the United States virtually the whole of its modern Pacific frontier. In 1863 construction started of

PREVIOUS PAGES: Commodore Matthew Perry comes ashore to sign the initial agreement with the Shogun's government, 8 March 1854.

ABOVE: Commodore Perry as seen by a Japanese artist.

ABOVE RIGHT: The California gold rush of 1849.

ABOVE, FAR RIGHT: American whalers in the Pacific, 1852.

FAR RIGHT: The meeting of the Central Pacific and Union Pacific Railroads in Utah, 10 May 1869.

RIGHT: A poster announcing the first American Transcontinental railroad service, 1869.

*The Japanese soon found that Samurai
swords and oriental diplomacy were no match
for Western naval technology.*

the Union Pacific and Central Pacific Railroads, and when the two ends met in Utah on 10 May 1869 the only 'frontier' left for Americans was the ocean itself.

This rapid expansion was achieved largely by the technology on which the Japanese had turned their backs. Just as the railroad allowed travel across continents, so the first practical ocean-going steamships, appearing at the end of the 1830s, made trade across the Pacific a reality. American whaling ships began to venture regularly into the Pacific (Melville's *Moby Dick* was written in 1851), and the Pacific Mail Steamship Company, founded in 1848, planned to open a regular route from San Francisco to Shanghai, the main trading port with China since the Opium War. Japan lay on the China route, and guarantees were needed for ships steaming to Japan of provisions, water, good treatment if in distress, and access to the (overestimated) Japanese coal stocks. After allowing the Shogunate a year to think through the implications of his visit, Perry returned in February 1854, and not surprisingly the Japanese signed a provisional agreement a month later, followed in July 1858 by a Treaty of Amity and Commerce with the United States, and in October by similar treaties with Britain, France, Imperial Russia and the Netherlands.

The Japanese soon found that Samurai swords and oriental diplomacy were no match for Western naval technology. On 14 August 1863 a British fleet of seven ships bombarded Kagoshima, capital of

the powerful Satsuma clan, in response to their failure to make reparations for what, to the Japanese, was the innocent action of killing a British citizen who had failed to show proper deference to a clan leader. In the following year the Japanese attempted to expel all foreigners, to be rewarded with another bombardment, of the Shimonoseki forts by an international fleet. In the face of this new reality, the death of the Emperor in 1867 was followed by the Boshin War (1868-9), a brief civil war which broke the power of the Shogunate, giving real authority to the new Emperor Mutsuhito in the *Ishin* ('Restoration,' or more accurately 'Renovation'). The Emperor transferred his capital to Edo, renamed *Tokyo* ('Eastern Capital') and took the reign-name of *Meiji* ('Enlightened Rule'). From then on, under the political slogans *fukoku kyohei* ('rich country, strong army') and *bunmei kaika* ('[eastern] civilization and [western] knowledge') Japan sought to escape the fate of China by copying Western ways.

Central to *fukoku kyohei* and Japan's control over its own future were an Army and a Navy organized along Western lines. Both were created in 1868 and made Departments of State in 1872, with conscription introduced a year later. The organization and training of the Army was copied from Imperial Germany, and that of the Navy from the British Royal Navy. The first ship, and the first ironclad, in the Japanese Imperial Navy were both American, the *Tsukuba*, a screw frigate of 1950 tons and 20 guns and the *Adsuma*, the old CSS *Stonewall Jackson* of Civil War fame. The first modern wooden vessel built in Japan itself was the *Seiki*, a despatch boat of 857 tons launched at Yokosuka in 1875. More importantly, as Imperial Japan began to transform itself into an industrial state, it commissioned from British

yards all-steel armored vessels with a speed of about 13 knots, the first being the *Fuso* of 3700 tons and four 9.4-inch guns in 1877. Eight years later Japan purchased from the British two of the new 'protected cruisers,' the *Naniwa* and *Takachiko* of 3000 tons, and began to build a sister ship for them. Launched in 1891, this was the *Hashidate*, the first armored warship to be built in Japan. For a country that less than 40 years before had seen nothing larger than a fishing boat it was an astonishing achievement. In 1872 the Japanese Imperial Navy consisted only of 17 ships, of which two were ironclads, totaling 14,000 tons. Building programs in 1882, 1886 and 1892 meant that by 1894 the Imperial Navy boasted 28 modern warships totaling 57,000 tons, plus 24 torpedo boats. In one generation, Japan had become a modern second-class naval power.

As often happens when societies face rapid change, many Japanese reacted by emphasizing 'traditional' cultural values. Old customs were codified – or even invented – for the first time only in the 1870s. Many classic works of Kabuki theater date from this period. Judo was invented in 1882 from a variety of Japanese wrestling styles, and karate was introduced from Okinawa a decade later. Even the worship of the Emperor was made official only in 1871. This mixture of old and new showed in the Japanese system of government. By the Meiji Constitution of 1889 the Emperor appointed the Prime Minister, who in turn picked his cabinet, but was expected

to take advice from the two-chamber Diet. The Privy Council of senior officials also advised the Emperor, together with members of the cabinet, at Imperial Conferences. By tradition the Emperor never spoke at these meetings, his thoughts being put forward by the Prime Minister. The Army Minister and Navy Minister were appointed directly by the Emperor, not the Prime Minister, from the highest ranks of their own services, meaning that often both ministers would defer to their respective senior commanders. Both services could in effect block the formation of a government by refusing to appoint a minister unless they approved of the rest of the cabinet. As a result, both the Army and Navy became heavily involved in politics, divided into factions in opposition to each other and to the government itself.

Moreover, by the Japanese tradition of *nemawashi* ('root binding'), major political decisions were reached very indirectly. The *zaibatsu*, the giant financial and industrial families, would expect to be consulted, as would the *mombatsu*, the senior bureaucrats, and until the later 1920s the *Genro*, senior statesmen out of office. Any government was also expected to act in accordance with *Kodo* ('the Imperial Way') and with *Yamato Damashii* ('the Spirit of Japan'), and because of this a belief in *gekokujo* was particularly strong in the armed forces. Meaning 'the low achieving dominance over the high,' this went back to the feudal idea of a vassal supplanting his lord, and translated as something between 'initiative' and 'insubordination.'

LEFT: The Emperor Meiji shortly after his accession to the throne.

BELOW LEFT: A Kabuki theater performance, one of the traditional Japanese arts given new life by the stress of change in the 1870s.

BELOW: Chinese torpedo boats attack Japanese warships during the Sino-Japanese War.

Gekokujo was not a moral crime, nor did it interfere with the strong bonds of loyalty and hierarchy in Japanese society. If a subordinate openly defied his superior and succeeded it was acknowledged as *karma* ('fate' is an inadequate translation). If he failed he might expect to be punished, but only according to how far he had acted in the spirit of *Kodo*. In this way, the Army or Navy might defy the government, and pursue totally different policies, with no sense of being at fault.

The Japanese attitude toward the West by the end of the nineteenth century contained many contradictions. Western technology was admired, and Western institutions and values were copied. But Japan, its traditional social structure founded on notions of 'face' and personal honor, found the experience of trying to gain acceptance as a major power a deeply humiliating one. By their own beliefs, the Japanese were a semi-divine people, ruled by an Emperor who was the direct descendant of the goddess *Amaterasu*. As such, the American concept of Manifest Destiny was very familiar to them as the perpetual and unchanging 'Mandate of Heaven,' the right and duty of the Japanese to extend the Emperor's rule over all inferior peoples.

Oddly, this belief was also confirmed by the latest in Western thinking. By the 1890s the notions of Charles Darwin, that species must compete to survive, had been translated into crude 'Social Darwinianism,' the identification of the main racial or political groups of mankind with separate species and the belief that they must fight for dominance. Distinctions of culture were seen as absolute barriers, and until quite recently intelligent people spoke of the 'White Race' in conflict with the 'Yellow Peril.' It was perhaps natural for the very unified culture of Japan to adopt these ideas. What is harder to understand is that they were commonplace even in the United States, a country founded on immigration and on the concept of equality for all.

The belief that they must copy the Western powers in a struggle for survival led the Japanese naturally toward China, where the Manchu Empire had shown itself weak in the face of Western pressure. Japan looked to China as a source of land, manpower, resources and markets, a basis for its own Empire in the East. What was then the farthest outpost of the Manchu Empire, the Korean peninsula, is at its closest only 30 miles from the Japanese island of Tsushima. Since 1636 Korea had been ruled by its own Emperor, with ill-defined vassal status toward China. In 1885 the Japanese secured from China the Treaty of Tientsin, by which all Chinese troops were withdrawn from Korea. When in 1894 the Chinese sent troops to halt a Korean insurrection, referring to it as their 'tributary state,' Japan used this as a pretext for confrontation.

The Sino-Japanese War of 1894-5 proved an almost embarrassingly easy Japanese victory. Fighting actually started with an encounter between Japanese and Chinese warships on 25 July 1894, followed by a formal Japanese declaration of war on 1 August. Contrary

to popular myth, it has been normal practice for centuries for fighting to start before an actual declaration of war. The first Japanese blows against China were in keeping both with Western customs of war and with Japanese attitudes. Even *bushido*, the code of the Samurai, recognized the *Iai*, the sword blow struck by surprise in a duel before the ritual salute to disable an opponent, as perfectly proper.

The decisive naval battle of the war, the Battle of the Yellow Sea, took place on 17 September 1894, in which 12 Japanese warships under Admiral Ito Yukyo encountered an equal number of Chinese warships under Admiral Ting and sank five of them without loss in five hours. Although lighter in overall tonnage, the Chinese ships were not, on paper, inferior to the Japanese, and their two largest battleships, *Chen Yuen* and *Ting Yuen*, were nearly twice the size of the *Yoshino*, Admiral Ito's flagship. The Japanese victory was one of superior seamanship, training, and weapons technology, and it kept the rest of the Chinese fleet in harbor until the end of the war.

The Japanese overran Korea, captured the main Chinese naval base of Port Arthur (modern Luda) and were threatening Tientsin and Peking by the time the Treaty of Shimonoseki was signed on 17 April 1895. China was forced to recognize Korean independence, to open up four more ports and the Yangtze River to Japanese trade, to negotiate a trade treaty – concluded in 1896 – granting Japan most favored nation status, to allow the Japanese to manufacture goods on Chinese soil, and to pay an indemnity, which the Japanese then used to build more battleships. China also gave up Formosa (Taiwan) and the Pescadore Islands, along with Port Arthur and the Kwantung peninsula on which it stood.

The Treaty of Shimonoseki had not even been ratified before Japan was taught a humiliating lesson in international power politics. In the 'Triple Intervention' the powers of France, Germany and Imperial Russia invited Japan, in courteous diplomatic language, to reconsider its demand for Port Arthur. To reinforce the point, there were 30,000 Russian troops in the Far East ready to come to China's aid. With the establishment of its Far Eastern naval base at Vladivostok the Russian Empire had also become a Pacific power, and all three countries had their own interests in China. The Japanese had little choice but to back down. It did not help matters that in 1896 the Russians forced China to grant them passage for the Trans-Siberian Railway across Manchuria to Vladivostok, and two years later themselves obtained a lease on Port Arthur as a naval base.

In 1895 the idea of Japan confronting Russia seemed absurd. But the Japanese were driven by a belief in their own racial superiority to offset simple numbers, by a desire to redress their national humiliation, by their need for the resources of China, and by an acceptance of *karma* – if the impossible had to be done, then they would do it. Spending on the Navy was increased from 9.5 million yen in 1891 to 58.5 million yen in 1898. By 1904 the Japanese Imperial Navy consisted of nine battleships, eight armored cruisers, 16 protected cruisers, 20 destroyers, 82 torpedo boats and 24 miscellaneous craft. The four biggest battleships, the Shikishima class, were, at over 15,000 tons, the largest warships then afloat, with a main armament of four 12-inch guns and a top speed of 18 knots.

Most of Japan's warships had been built in British yards, and the two countries had maintained good relations partly through Japan's copying of Royal Navy ideas. As the result of an event from which Japan could not have been more remote, the Second Boer War of 1899-1902, Britain decided that its policy of 'Glorious Isolation' from alliances with other states was no longer wise and, as an indirect move back into the international fold, chose to conclude its first peacetime alliance for nearly a century with the Japanese. By the Treaty of London of 30 January 1902 Britain and Japan agreed that if either fought a war with only one enemy in the Far East then the other would stand neutral, but if the war involved two enemies then Britain and Japan would fight together. The Anglo-Japanese Alliance made such humiliations as the Triple Intervention a thing of the past for the Japanese. If war came with Russia, then no other country could intervene without confronting the British Empire.

This would have mattered less to the United States had it not been for a shift in American political and strategic thinking that came about just as the Japanese made their first moves against China. Virtually immune from invasion, United States naval strategy had since the Civil War (1861-65) been based on the use of fast commerce raiders to disrupt enemy trade and on static monitors to defend its ports. Not until 1883 did the United States build its first four steel warships – the 'ABCD' protected cruisers, *Atlanta*, *Boston*, *Chicago* and *Dolphin*, of 4500 tons. Between 1885 and 1889 30 warships were authorized, including two second-class battleships of 7000 tons each. Then in 1890 a professor at the Naval War College, Captain (later Admiral) Alfred T Mahan, produced his book *The Influence of Sea Power Upon History 1660-1783*, which was to dominate naval thinking for a generation.

Mahan, who may have invented the term 'sea-power,' took as his model the success of the Royal Navy and British Empire. He argued that to be powerful and prosperous a nation – such as the United States – must engage in global trade, and have a large merchant fleet for the purpose. In time of war it needed to guarantee safe passage for its own merchant ships and those of neutral countries. This meant battleships capable of driving off any blockading enemy force. For the future, an even stronger US Navy might blockade enemy ports and control trade routes across the globe, for which it would need naval bases and coaling stations. Mahan placed great stress on the decisive battle, the clash of battleships that would determine command of the seas.

Mahan's ideas were taken up by the 'American Imperialists,' politicians who believed in Manifest Destiny just as firmly as the Japanese believed in the Mandate of Heaven. These men viewed the remains of the Spanish Empire in the Caribbean and Pacific as a suitable target for expansion, and on 20 April 1898 the United States declared war against a hopelessly inferior Spain. The main land theater was Cuba, although the presence of three of the four new US Navy battleships in the North Atlantic prevented Spanish reinforcements reaching the island after the main Spanish fleet was smashed at the Battle of Santiago on 3 July. To take part, the battleship *Oregon* steamed round Cape Horn from the Pacific, a distance of 13,000 nautical miles, or more than twice the distance from California to Japan. Meanwhile in the Philippines, Commodore George Dewey with the US Navy's Asiatic Squadron of four cruisers and two gunboats destroyed the small Spanish fleet at anchor in Manila Bay on 1 May.

By the Treaty of Paris of 10 December 1898 the United States annexed from Spain the islands of Cuba and Puerto Rico, together with Wake, Guam and the Philippines, for which it paid compensation. Almost as an afterthought, the Hawaiian Islands, where in 1891 American forces had supported an overthrow of the monarchy and the establishment of a republic, were also annexed. This moved the 'frontier' roughly 5000 miles into the Pacific, and meant that for the first time the Americans had taken responsibility for territories that they had no intention of making part of the Union. The Philippines were also completely indefensible by any means that the United States had available. Their possession meant that if Japan were to expand southward then the two countries would inevitably come into conflict. The seeds of conflict over China were sown a year later, in 1899, when the United States proposed its

TOP LEFT: Land fighting in Korea during the Sino-Japanese War.

TOP: The Battle of Manila Bay, showing the American Asiatic Squadron destroying the Spanish fleet, May 1898.

ABOVE: American warships at the Battle of Santiago, July 1898.

'Open Door' policy, that all nations should be allowed to trade with – and exploit – China equally, based on the fact that there was nothing in China crucial to American needs. This meant that the United States would not only oppose Japanese expansion into China, but do so from a point of moralizing detachment that the Japanese found both insulting and hypocritical.

In autumn 1901 President William McKinley was assassinated, bringing unexpectedly to the White House his Vice-President, Theodore Roosevelt, who had served as Assistant Secretary of the Navy before the Spanish-American War. True to Mahan's principles, Roosevelt pushed through Congress in the next four years authorization for 10 first-class battleships, four armored cruisers, and 17 other warships, a total of more than 250,000 tons of shipping. In 1903, after the government of Colombia refused to sell the United States land for a canal through the isthmus of Panama, Roosevelt backed a revolt leading to the creation of an independent Panama,

which in turn granted control of the canal to the United States. Work began on the canal in 1904 and it was opened 10 years later. Roosevelt's far-sighted fear was of a future naval war with Germany in the Atlantic and Japan in the Pacific, for which the United States would need a strong navy in both oceans. He and others like him also saw the dawn of a new 'Pacific Era' following the Atlantic and Mediterranean eras, in which dominance of the Pacific would determine world power.

At the start of the twentieth century, relations between Japan and the United States in the Pacific were reasonably good, with their troops fighting side by side in the International Force which supressed the Boxer Rising in China in 1900. But the future likelihood of a clash with the United States was considerably increased by Japan's unexpected victory in the Russo-Japanese War of 1904-5. The pretext for this war was once again Korea, the independence of which Japan had guaranteed by the Treaty of Shimoneseki and which the Japanese claimed

LEFT: American troops in the Philippines shortly after the Spanish-American War.

BELOW LEFT: President Theodore Roosevelt in 1902.

RIGHT: President Theodore Roosevelt watches the building of the Panama Canal, November 1906.

BELOW: American troops defending their legation in Peking during the Boxer Rising of 1900.

*Of 38 Imperial Russian ships at Tsushima
19 were sunk, seven were captured, two were
scuttled and the rest dispersed.*

was under threat from Russian troops. Again, the wider issue was how much of a free hand Japan would be allowed in China. The Japanese, true to their traditions, began the war with a night attack on 8 February 1904 by destroyers and torpedo boats against the Russian Pacific Fleet in Port Arthur, crippling three of the seven battleships at anchor. The effect of the surprise attack, as the Japanese Commander-in-Chief Admiral Togo Heihachiro had hoped, was to shake Russian faith in the war and impose on the Pacific Fleet a policy of extreme caution. The formal Japanese declaration of war came on 10 February – in fact, Japan later argued that the war's first shots had been fired by a Russian gunboat in Korean waters late on 8 February.

While the Japanese were victorious in their land campaigns, the Russian Pacific Fleet did not sortie in earnest from Port Arthur until 10 August. The resulting Battle of Round Island was a Japanese victory, the Russian commander, Admiral V K Vitgeft, going down with his flagship the *Tsarevich*. After Port Arthur had fallen, the Russian Baltic Fleet (renamed the Second Pacific Fleet), which had sailed

half way round the world to reach Vladivostok, was engaged by Togo on 27 May 1905 at the Battle of Tsushima and annihilated. Of 38 Imperial Russian ships (including seven battleships), 19 were sunk, seven were captured, two scuttled themselves, and the remainder dispersed, some seeking internment in neutral ports. Only two destroyers and a cruiser reached safety at Vladivostok. Togo's fleet lost just three torpedo boats sunk, and none of his four battleships or eight cruisers was seriously damaged.

The war was ended by the Treaty of Portsmouth (New Hampshire) on 5 September 1905. Imperial Russia surrendered to Japan its lease on Port Arthur, control of southern Manchuria and the southern half of Sakhalin Island, and recognized the independence of Korea. To complete the Japanese victory, shortly before the treaty was signed the Anglo-Japanese Alliance was renewed for a further 10 years. Even so, when Togo's flagship, the *Mikasa*, blew up at anchor a week later, it was rumored to have been scuttled by Japanese officers unable to stand the disgrace. Imperial Russia had flatly refused to pay a Japanese indemnity demand of $60

LEFT: Admiral Togo Heihachiro at the time of the Russo-Japanese War.

BELOW LEFT: German troops in China during the Boxer Rising, joined by French, Russian, Italian, Japanese, Indian and Chinese soldiers and sailors.

ABOVE RIGHT: The *Orel*, one of the few Russian battleships to survive the Battle of Tsushima, showing the effects of Japanese gunnery.

RIGHT: Russian warships under fire during the Battle of Round Island.

ABOVE: The *Orel* shown before the Battle of Tsushima.

million, and the Japanese delegation had at last accepted this. So great was Japanese pride that many regarded this as a national humiliation. It was not encouraging for anyone trying to negotiate with Japan in the future.

This was a bad time for the United States to decide that the Yellow Peril was unwelcome on its shores. In 1906, the State of California tried to halt immigration from Japan, and the Japanese uproar at their treatment as an inferior race produced open talk of war. At the end of 1906 the Japanese Army, for the first time, included in its long-term plans a possible expansion southward toward the Philippines, and the Imperial Navy listed the United States as, after Russia, its most likely future opponent. The US Army and Navy also drew up 'Plan Orange,' an outline war plan against Japan.

In the middle of this, President Roosevelt decided on something between a show of strength and a show of pride. His new Navy was mainly concentrated in the Atlantic (known for historic reasons as the 'White Squadron'). In 1907 he ordered a Pacific cruise for the entire battleship fleet of 16 ships. The 'Great White Fleet' visited New Zealand on 10 August 1908 and Australia 10 days later. Bowing to the inevitable, Japan also issued an invitation, and on 18 October the American ships tied up alongside 16 Japanese ships in a display of equality.

Once more, only three years after the greatest Japanese naval victory, American warships, largely unwanted, rode at anchor in Tokyo Bay. Meanwhile, in February 1908 the Japanese and Americans reached the 'Gentleman's Agreement' on a quota system of immigration, leading on 30 November to the Root-Takahira Agreement, an exchange of notes rather than a formal treaty, in which both sides agreed to respect the existing situation in the Pacific, and on the Open Door policy toward China.

When Commodore Perry steamed into Edo Bay the first clash between armored warships was some 10 years in the future. Since then, warship development had accelerated at a dramatic pace. In 1906 the British Royal Navy produced the first truly modern battleship, HMS *Dreadnought*. Running on steam turbines, the *Dreadnought* at 17,900 tons had a maximum speed of 21 knots, and a main armament of 10 12-inch guns. With this speed and firepower, it was the equal of two or three existing battleships. The British followed this a year later with HMS *Invincible*, the world's first battlecruiser, less heavily armored than a battleship but mounting eight 12-inch guns and capable of 25 knots.

Within two years of Tsushima the whole of Togo's fleet, and every other battle fleet in the world, had suddenly become obsolete. The result was a massive worldwide race to build warships.

TOP RIGHT: The Russian flagship *Borodino* sinking at the Battle of Tsushima.

ABOVE RIGHT: The world's first modern battleship, HMS *Dreadnought*.

RIGHT: The world's first battle-cruiser, HMS *Invincible*.

The first American dreadnought, USS *Delaware*, was laid down in 1906, followed by six more in the next two years. By the time Roosevelt left office in 1909 the US Navy totaled 496,000 tons, or four times as much as in 1901. The first Japanese dreadnoughts, *Kawachi* and *Setsu*, were launched in 1910 and 1911, and in 1913 came Japan's first battle-cruiser, the British-built *Kongo*, which was also the last Japanese capital ship built outside Japan itself. In the same year the British raised the stakes again by starting HMS *Queen Elizabeth*, first of a class of five battleships of 27,500 tons with eight 15-inch guns and a top speed of 24 knots.

Japan, meanwhile, was free of its last restraints. In 1910, dropping any pretence at Korean independence, the Japanese annexed the country after a secret deal with the Russians. In the following year the trade treaties imposed in 1858 finally lapsed, and equal treaties were signed instead. By this time Japan was an industrialized nation of some 50 million people, desperate for markets and resources, proud of its own achievements. In the next 20 years, Japanese industrial production increased by almost 200 percent, and foreign trade by 100 percent.

Meanwhile, the high costs of military rearmament and the naval arms race produced an open challenge to the Japanese government from both the Army and Navy. In September 1911 the Imperial Navy announced its 'Eight-Eight' program – eight new battleships and eight battle-cruisers to be built before 1918. The government could find less than a quarter of the money needed, and was forced to resign. In May 1912, for the first time, a general and former Army Minister became Prime Minister, demanding an increase in the size of the Army. Again the government resigned, and when another general was appointed as Prime Minister the Navy refused to nominate a Navy Minister. The crisis was finally resolved by a deal between the Army and the Navy in February 1913. Both services would, however, clash in the future.

In the midst of this open fight for power the Emperor Meiji died on 30 July 1912, to be succeeded by his son Yoshihito, who took the title *Taisho* ('Great Righteousness'). Meiji's reign of 45 years had seen the transformation of Japan into a major power. In less than 30 years, the Japanese would gamble that power at Pearl Harbor in a bid for domination of the Pacific world.

CHAPTER TWO

THE SEARCH
FOR PEACE

IN 1909, accepting that the Philippines could not be defended by warships, the US Navy began the construction of its main base in the Pacific at Pearl Harbor, close to Honolulu on Oahu in the Hawaiian Islands, 3000 miles from Manila and over 2000 miles from the continental United States. The overwhelming strength of the US Navy, including all its battleships, was still in the Atlantic. The Pacific Fleet (officially designated as such in 1917) consisted of a few cruisers, together with the Asiatic Squadron to protect US interests in China. Through the agreements imposed on the Manchu Empire, foreign warships were permitted into Chinese ports or along navigable rivers to protect traders or missionaries in the interior. Indeed, for most Americans, reports from missionaries formed the major source of information on China for the next 20 years, inevitably reinforcing the highly moralizing tone taken by the United States over Japanese intervention in China.

Increasingly, the United States had come to accept Japan as its most likely enemy in the Pacific. In 1911 War Plan Orange was revised in detail, revealing the weakness of the American position when confronting the Japanese. This was followed in 1913 by another war scare, again started by the State of California, which passed on 15 April legislation forbidding 'aliens ineligible to citizenship,' including all Asiatics, from owning land (second generation Japanese Americans, or *Nisei*, were allowed to apply for citizenship). With the Panama Canal not yet completed and the *Kongo* about to sail from Britain, the timing could not have been worse. The government of President Woodrow Wilson, including Franklin D Roosevelt as Assistant Secretary of the Navy, worked to avoid a war with Japan while recognizing that the Pacific Fleet must be strengthened. Wilson, like Theodore Roosevelt, had to fight the traditional isolationist attitude of many members of

the legislature, especially those from land-locked states.

Surprisingly, therefore, when Japan and the United States next went to war it was on the same side. On 15 August 1914, as World War I was starting in Europe, Japan presented Imperial Germany with an effective declaration of war by demanding from it the lease of the Chinese treaty port of Tsingtao, in a document consciously modeled on the Triple Intervention. This was very much a gesture of support for Great Britain, following the second renewal of the Anglo-Japanese Alliance in 1911. Japanese and British troops together seized Tsingtao on 7 November, by which time the Japanese had also occupied the German owned Marshall, Mariana and Caroline Islands. Japanese destroyers escorted Australian and New Zealand troops to the Near East, and a destroyer squadron was even sent to the Mediterranean to assist the British in 1915.

The political situation in China by this

PAGES 22-23: President Woodrow Wilson (center) with his staff at the Paris peace talks following World War I.

LEFT: Senior officers of the major powers' Asiatic naval contingents on board the Japanese Asiatic Squadron flagship in Chinese waters, 1932.

ABOVE: The battleships USS *Ohio* and USS *Missouri* passing through the Panama Canal, 1915.

BELOW: Japanese sailors, together with American and Czech soldiers, marching through Vladivostok, 1918.

time was extremely complex. In 1911 the old Manchu Empire had at last collapsed, and a Chinese Republic was proclaimed. In practice, although most Western countries recognized the Republic as the government of China, it controlled only eastern China, with the rest of the country split into semi-independent war-lordships, each about as big as a medium-sized American state. On 18 January 1915 Japan, taking advantage of the fact that the European powers were fully en-gaged at war, presented the Chinese Re-public with a list of 'Twenty-One Demands,' by which China was to give up Tsingtao, extend Japanese rights in Manchuria, to accept Japanese domina-tion of its industry and commerce, and even allow Japanese 'advisers' in senior political, military and administrative posts. After negotiation, a version of the Twenty-One Demands was accepted by the Chinese Republic on 9 April. But next year the Republic itself collapsed, to be replaced by the Chinese Nationalists (*Kuomintang*), who themselves declared war on Germany on 14 August 1917 in an effort to put China on the winning side for the peace settlement.

Initially, the United States stood neu-tral from World War I, showing its tradi-tional isolationism. As the war grew in intensity and scope, however, Congress passed the Navy Act of 29 August 1916, authorizing the construction within three years of 10 battleships, six battle-cruisers, and 141 smaller craft and sub-marines at a cost of $300 million, in effect a completely new US Navy. Eventually, on 2 April 1917, the United States en-tered the war against Germany, contri-buting five battleships to help the Royal Navy in the Atlantic. In November 1917 Japan and the United States reached the Lansing-Ishii Agreement, another ex-change of diplomatic notes in which the United States, while reaffirming the Open Door policy, recognized Japan's 'special interests' in China.

In November 1917 the Russian Empire collapsed into civil war from which the new Soviet Union emerged three years later. In response, the Japanese and British landed troops at Vladivostok in 1918 to support anti-Soviet forces in Siberia. The United States also contri-

*The Imperial Japanese Navy's flagship,
the* Nagato, *was, at 38,500 tons, the
world's largest battleship.*

buted troops to the Siberian expedition, but refused any cooperation with the Japanese, who responded in kind. Japanese troops did not finally withdraw from Vladivostok until October 1922, and Japan used the chaos in Russia to annex the northern half of Sakhalin Island, giving the country for the first time its own oilfields.

In 1919 the multiple treaties of the Peace of Paris, ending World War I, granted Japan control of Tsingtao, to the disgust of China, which refused to accept the treaties. The newly-formed League of Nations, intended to keep the peace for the future, also granted Japan trusteeship over the Marshalls, Carolinas and Marianas, so putting a belt of Japanese territory between Pearl Harbor and the Philippines. This was just one of the many reasons which led the United States to reject both the Peace of Paris and the League, and to retreat once more into isolation.

It is hard to overstate the impact of World War I on the Western powers. British and American political tradition saw foreign policy as an extension of personal morality, and war as a great moral evil (or, from the other side, as a moral crusade). Now, the immense destruction and human loss of World War I left a conviction that even the threat of armed force was morally repugnant, that such a war must never again be allowed to happen, and that the way to peace was through disarmament and negotiation. Even 'Empire' became a slightly dirty word, as the victors accepted League of Nations trusteeships rather than outright annexation.

Conveniently, perhaps, this recognition that modern, industrial war was too destructive to have any worthwhile purpose came at the moment when the Western nations, particularly the United States and Great Britain, were at their most powerful compared to the rest of the world. To Japan, never heavily involved in the war, the Western attitude seemed nothing but hypocisy. As an overpopulated, industrialized country in need of resources Japan was doing nothing that the United States had not done a century before. Nevertheless, unlike the Americans, the Japanese willingly joined the League of Nations as a founder member in January 1920, despite failing to get a declaration of racial equality placed in its charter.

In 1914 the Japanese government at last agreed to the Imperial Navy's Eight-Eight program, only to find once more that it was beyond the country's financial

reach. In 1917 the program was trimmed to Eight-Four, increasing to Eight-Six a year later. The full Eight-Eight program, planned to take eight years, was not adopted until 1920. At this date the Royal Navy was still the largest in the world at 4,153,000 tons (apart from torpedo boats, gunboats and minor vessels), but many of its larger ships were elderly veterans of active service in World War I, in need of replacement. The US Navy in 1920 was 1,370.000 tons, with a further 820,000 tons planned for 1924. The Japanese Imperial Navy, third largest in the world, was 686,000 tons, with the Eight-Eight program adding another 946,000 tons. In keeping with Japanese 'face,' the Imperial Navy's flagship was the world's largest battleship, the *Nagato* of 38,500 tons.

The prospect of a new naval arms race, particularly after the strain of World War I, was too much for the United States. Backed by the White Dominions of the Pacific – chiefly Canada – the Americans pressured the British into giving up the Anglo-Japanese Alliance, due for renewal in August 1923, in return for a wider agreement between the major powers. The Japanese, who had prized their alliance with Britain, attended the Washington Conference, which began on 2 November 1921, only with reluctance. Within two days of the start of the conference, Prime Minister Hara Kei was assassinated in Tokyo, possibly in protest over the decision.

At the Washington Conference, a Four-Power Pact was signed on 13 December by Britain, France, Japan and the United States, agreeing to respect each other's rights and possessions in the Far East. The conference then concentrated on naval matters, and after two months produced an agreement that no new battleships were to be built for 10 years. By 1931 Great Britain and the United States were each to have 15 battleships totaling 525,000 tons, and Japan nine battleships totaling 315,000 tons, in the proportions 5:5:3 (plus 1.67 for the French and Italians). Battleships were limited to 35,000 tons with 16-inch guns and other ships to 10,000 tons with 8-inch guns. No naval bases were to be constructed closer to Japan than Singapore and Pearl Harbor, leaving Manila and Hong Kong undefended. This was agreed by the Five-Power Naval Treaty of 6 February 1922, together with the Nine-Power Pact on the same day, including China, Belgium, the Netherlands and Portugal, which confirmed the sovereignty and territorial integrity of

China, while supporting the Open Door.

The Japanese, who had wanted a 10:10:7 ratio, giving them another 50,000 tons, came away from Washington without realizing that, to preserve peace, the United States had shown remarkable restraint. Whereas the Eight-Eight program was crippling Japan economically, the Americans could easily have afforded their new Navy. The Japanese were also insulted that the Anglo-Japanese Alliance, to which they had proved so loyal, was discarded so readily, and angered by once again being treated as an inferior people. The French, in particular, made little effort to disguise their view that the real American purpose was – as an American report put it with shocking frankness – 'to marshal the white world for an inevitable conflict with the yellow races.' The Washington Conference marked the end of Japan's friendship with Great Britain, and the start of a growing British dependence on the United States.

As well as battleships, the Washington Conference was also forced to consider two new kinds of sea power that had emerged from World War I – the submarine and the aircraft carrier. The first practical submarine appeared in 1901, and by 1904 Japan had 13 boats. But it was the invention of the diesel engine a year later that turned the submarine into a true ocean-going craft, as the Germans demonstrated in World War I with their U-Boat campaign. By 1918 the largest US Navy submarine, at 569 tons, had a range of 4000 miles at 14 knots, and the British submarine fleet numbered 131 vessels. The Washington Conference found it impossible, however, to reach agreement on these boats.

The role of aircraft at sea developed equally swiftly. The first flight by the Wright brothers took place on 17 December 1903, but already by 1914 a few nations possessed seaplane tenders, including the Japanese *Wakamiya* at Tsingtao. A British seaplane tender, HMS *Engadine*, was present at the Battle of Jutland on 31 May 1916, the one major naval battle of the war. By the fall of 1913 the Royal Navy had perfected the dropping of torpedoes from aircraft, and on 12 August 1915 two Short 184 seaplanes of the Royal Naval Air Service successfully torpedoed Turkish merchant ships in the Sea of Marmara. Experiments over the next two years showed that it was possible for aircraft to take off and land from a flight deck, and on 19 July 1918 seven Royal Air Force Sopwith Camels, launched from

ABOVE: One of the earliest British aircraft carriers, HMS *Hermes*, launched in 1919, shown off the China coast in 1931.

Britain's first true aircraft carrier, HMS *Furious*, carried out a bombing raid against the airship sheds at Tondern in Germany. By the end of 1918 the Royal Navy was planning its 'Cuckoo Raid,' an attack by Sopwith Cuckoo torpedo bombers from three aircraft carriers against the German High Seas Fleet in harbor, which if it had taken place would have pre-empted Pearl Harbor by more than 20 years.

From the 1920s onward there was considerable disagreement in the world's major navies between officers who still measured sea power in terms of battleships and big guns, and others – by no

means always young or junior – who argued that carriers and land-based aircraft, armed with bombs and torpedoes, had decisively changed sea warfare. The problem for each country was whether to risk, at tremendous cost, changing its main naval weapon for one which, whatever its promise, had never been tried in war. That most navies were still thinking in terms of battleships in 1941 was largely due to this 'wait and see' attitude.

In July 1921, in response to the common jibe that 'aircraft can't sink battleships,' Brigadier-General 'Billy' Mitchell of the US Army Air Service showed that they could, by sinking the 22,440 ton

RIGHT: An early Royal Navy experiment in launching an aircraft over the front turret of the cruiser HMS *Africa* in 1912.

> *One Japanese officer who showed an unfashionable interest in aircraft in this period was Yamamoto Isoroku.*

ABOVE LEFT: Bombs falling around the *Ostfriesland* during bombing trials in 1921.

ABOVE: The USS *Lexington,* shown during World War II.

ABOVE RIGHT: Admiral Yamamoto Isoroku at about the time of Pearl Harbor.

LEFT: A white phosphorus bomb exploding over the deck of USS *Alabama* during bombing trials in 1923.

former German battleship *Ostfriesland* with shore-based planes. The battleship lobby replied that *Ostfriesland* had been a hulk with no anti-bomb deck armor, no damage-control crews, and no anti-aircraft defenses (much like a ship caught by surprise in home port, in fact!), and that Mitchell's test proved nothing. In fact, at sea, carrying ammunition and with full steam up, the ship would have been even more vulnerable, although much harder to hit. Two years later Mitchell followed up his experiment by sinking the decommissioned battleship USS *Alabama* from the air. Mitchell's experiments led, by the end of the 1920s, to the accepted belief that heavy shore-based bombers, attacking from high altitudes, might pose a serious threat to ocean-going warships.

It was a different story with aircraft carriers, which were only gradually accepted by the more conservative admirals as having a role in supporting the battle fleet. Some admirals of the Imperial Navy made it a point of honor not to learn to fly, and to discourage their subordinates from flying. The Japanese war plan against the United States remained the *Kantai Kessen*, the great all-out battle in the Pacific as popularized by Mahan. The Imperial Navy would lie in wait while the American fleet came west from Pearl Harbor, losing ships on its way to harrassing attacks from Japanese submarines and aircraft, until the great clash of battleships decided the issue, much as at Tsushima.

The Washington Five Power Naval Treaty included aircraft carriers, as well as battleships, in a 5:5:3 ratio (with 2.22

for France and Italy), the British and Americans being allowed 135,000 carrier tons and the Japanese 81,000, with no carrier larger than 27,000 tons. This was indeed generous to the Japanese, who did not possess a single carrier at the time, launching their first, the *Hosho*, in December 1922. The terms of the treaty also allowed for battle-cruisers of up to 33,000 tons already being built on both sides of the Pacific, such as the *Akagi* or the USS *Lexington*, to be converted to aircraft carriers. In fact the *Lexington* and her sister ship the *Saratoga* both topped 36,000 tons when they entered service in 1928.

One Japanese officer who showed an unfashionable interest in aircraft in this period was also well placed to understand the United States, having studied at Harvard (like a number of his contemporaries) between 1919 and 1921. He was born Takano Isoroku in 1884, but in 1914 had been adopted into the Yamamoto family as Yamamoto Isoroku. He served as an instructor at the Imperial Naval Air College and as adjutant of the Naval Air Training School between 1921 and 1924, and as naval attaché in Washington between 1925 and 1927. 'Anyone who has seen the automobile factories of Detroit and the oilfields of Texas', Yamamoto wrote, 'knows that Japan lacks the national strength for a naval race with America.' Unusually, also, Yamamoto understood that 'the 5:5:3 ratio works well for us – it is a treaty to restrict the *other* parties.' It was this man, who both admired and feared the United States, who would draw up the plan for Pearl Harbor.

a power vacuum in which the government fell increasingly under the influence of the 'patriotic societies,' semi-secret organizations of extreme nationalists such as the *Kokuhonsha* ('National Foundation Society'), whose members included three future prime ministers, and the *Sakurakai* ('Cherry Society') of senior Army officers. These men talked freely of the need for a *Showa Ishin*, a 'Restoration' or increase of Japanese power as great as that seen under Meiji, backed by a spiritual reawakening of the Japanese people to their new destiny.

In China, meanwhile, the *Kuomintang* under its leader Generalissimo Chiang Kai-shek had by 1925 established itself as the National Government, and a year later began its military campaign to unify the country. This was contrary to the ambitions of the Japanese Army, which increasingly pursued its own policy remote from the government, even forcing the resignation of Prime Minister Tanaka Giichi in 1928. On a day-to-day basis, power was exercised more and more by the 'five ministers' – Foreign, Finance, Army, Navy and the Prime Minister, with the Emperor's authorization a formality. Japan already took some 35 percent of China's trade, and with the Japanese population increasing by roughly one million a year, the world recession following the Wall Street crash of 1929 greatly strengthened the Army's demands for a Japanese empire in Asia.

At the Geneva Naval Conference of 1927, called to review the progress of the Washington Naval Treaty, the Japanese again pressed for a 10:10:7 ratio, but no agreement was reached. A year later in Paris came the high point of the search for peace: the Kellogg-Briand Pact, signed by Japan, the United States and 27 other nations, all renouncing the use of war except in defense of their own frontiers – an exception which was open to wide interpretation. On 21 January 1930, a year before the Washington Naval Treaty was due to expire, a further naval conference was called in London, with Captain Yamamoto among the Japanese delegates. The militant 'Fleet' faction of the Imperial Navy under Chief of Staff Admiral Kanjii Kato pressed the government to demand parity with Britain and the United States, but Prime Minister Hamaguchi Osachi, supported by moderates like Yamamoto, refused to ask for more than the 10:10:7 ratio. By the London Naval Treaty of 1930, which was to last until 1936, the Japanese were granted a ratio of 100:100:69.75, a fraction less than their demands.

On 25 December 1926 the Emperor Taisho died, to be replaced by his son Hirohito, who took the reign-name *Showa* ('Shining Peace'). It was an optimistic choice rather than a prophetic one. As with the death of Meiji, there was the sense of an era ending, and this one also ended in conflict between the Japanese government, the Army and the Navy, and in hostility from the United States. In April 1923, in the face of continuing Japanese military pressure on China, the Americans tore up the Lansing-Ishii Agreement, arguing that they had meant to support only Japanese economic interests in China, not its political ambitions. This was followed on 1 July 1924 by the Quota Immigration Act, which in practice banned all immigration from Japan, and a year later by the first major exercises of the US Pacific

Fleet, including battleships, in a test of War Plan Orange.

In the same year, the Imperial Navy began building four cruisers which at over 12,000 tons violated the Washington Naval Treaty, a fact which it kept successfully hidden from the Americans. A year later, fearful of war with the Soviet Union, the Japanese government, despite fierce protests from both the Army and Navy, returned the northern half of Sakhalin Island with its oil to the Soviets in return for their recognition of the 1905 Treaty of Portsmouth, including the presence of Japanese troops – the Kwantung Army – at Port Arthur and on the Kwantung peninsula.

By the end of the 1920s almost all the *Genro*, the old politicians who had advised the Emperor since the Meiji Restoration, had died or retired, leaving

LEFT: Emperor Hirohito attending a parade shortly after his accession to the throne.

Once more, this was quite generous to Japan, given that Britain had 43 capital ships, the United States had 33 afloat or building, and Japan only had 18. Nevertheless, Admiral Kanjii resigned in protest at the treaty on 10 June. The Navy Minister, Admiral Takarabe Takeshi, who had headed the London negotiations, was also forced to resign on 3 October, and the Imperial Navy only agreed to appoint his successor in return for what became known as the 'first supplemental building program,' the construction of four new cruisers over five years. With feelings running very high, on 14 November a patriotic society member gunned down Prime Minister Hamaguchi in public. He died of his wounds nine months later. In March 1931 an attempt by the *Sakurakai* society to install a military government was only

narrowly called off by the Army itself, and the plotters went unpunished.

Then, on 18 September, came the Liutaiokoan Incident in Manchuria, a pretext for the Kwantung Army to occupy Mukden (modern Shenyang), giving Japan control of Manchuria. The Chinese response at having a province of their country occupied was to boycott Japanese trade, leading to the Japanese seizure by force of Shanghai, the main Chinese trading port. On 18 February 1932 Japan transformed Manchuria into the independent state of Manchukuo under the Emperor Pu Yi (who had also been the last Manchu Emperor of China), as a Japanese puppet – a clear breach of the Washington Nine-Power Treaty. China appealed to the League of Nations, which in October 1932 produced the Lytton Commission Report, rejecting

ABOVE: Generalissimo Chiang Kai-shek at the time of the Japanese intervention in Manchuria.

RIGHT: Prince Takamatsu of Japan being greeted by Emperor Pu Yi on his arrival in Manchukuo in 1932.

Japan's claim of Manchukuo's independence. In February 1933, when the League accepted the Lytton version, Japan left the League in protest, arguing that League rules applied 'only to organized states, not to anarchies like China – there is no such thing as a responsible Chinese government.' Later that year Japanese Army forces probed across the Great Wall into northern China itself.

For the first time, a major act of Japanese foreign policy had been carried out by the Army independently of the government. Indeed, with the assassination of another Prime Minister, Inukai Tsuyoshi, on 15 May 1932, civilian government in Japan broke down. In the next nine years there would be nine governments, of which six would be led by generals or admirals, in what an American observer called 'government by assassination.' A year later Japan was threatened with another military coup, the *shinpeitai* ('divine soldiers') plot, which again failed at the last minute, leaving the plotters virtually unpunished. Even the Emperor, who expressed quiet doubts about the actions

launched in his name, was not entirely safe from such plots.

This military domination was disastrous for the Japanese economy. Between 1933 and 1937 Japanese funding of the armed forces increased from 30 percent of all government spending to 70 percent, and the more was spent the more was demanded. The 'second supplemental building program,' begun in 1934, would give Japan by 1937 two smaller aircraft carriers to go with the *Akagi* and her sister ship the *Kaga*. It also made things very much harder for Japanese diplomats overseas, who were often not informed of military plans. On 17 April 1934 the Japanese government issued the so-called 'Amo statement,' demanding that Japan must be allowed a free hand in reuniting China, without the intervention of other powers. In response, Germany, Italy and the United States sent assistance to the Chinese Nationalist forces. A long-term dispute began between the Japanese Army, which wished to expand into China, and the Navy, which looked southward toward Indochina and the Far East.

The situation in Japan was in marked

contrast to the United States, where in January 1933 Franklin D Roosevelt began what was to become an unprecedented 12 years as President, giving American foreign policy toward the Japanese considerable continuity. Roosevelt's immediate concern was to pull the United States out of the great economic depression, but the foreign position he inherited was hardly satisfactory. The United States possessed a skeleton Army and a Pacific Fleet considerably weaker than its Japanese opponents. Failure to build even the ships allowed by the Washington Treaty meant that the 1934 ratio between the US Navy and Imperial Navy was 10:8 and not 10:7 as permitted. On 16 June 1933 Congress passed the so-called Vinson Act, allowing Roosevelt $238 million to spend on the Navy, chiefly to replace elderly destroyers and submarines. But even as Japan threatened in the Far East, in Europe Chancellor Adolf Hitler announced Germany's departure from the League of Nations in 1933, and a year later began his new rearmament program. For political reasons Roosevelt took rearmament very slowly indeed.

THE DOORMAT

*'It is doubtful if air attacks can
be launched against Oahu in the face
of strong defensive aviation.'*

LEFT: A British newspaper cartoon of 1932 depicting the helplessness of the League of Nations in the face of Japanese aggression.

ABOVE: The prototype of the Boeing B-17 Flying Fortress, first flown in 1935. The fuselage blisters were later dropped from the design.

In the decade since the first experiments, meanwhile, the aircraft carrier had become a fully functioning weapons system. The Japanese Imperial Navy used carrier planes to bomb Shanghai on 28 January 1931 in support of the Army. More remarkably, the 1932 US Navy maneuvers, in which most of the fleet assembled in the Pacific, demonstrated what carriers could do by themselves. Admiral Harry E Yarnell, instead of keeping all three of his carriers with the fleet of 29 battleships and cruisers at 18 knots, used *Lexington* and *Saratoga*, escorted by destroyers, as a fast carrier group capable of 35 knots. Hard to detect behind a bad weather front, these carriers approached from the north to within 60 miles of the Hawaiian Islands, and at dawn on Sunday flew off an airstrike that caught Pearl Harbor by surprise. It was a good prediction of the Japanese attack nine years later. Even so, the official conclusion was that 'it is doubtful if air attacks can be launched against Oahu in the face of strong defensive aviation without subjecting carriers to the danger of material damage.' In the April 1937 maneuvers, a similar attack was made on Pearl Harbor without significant loss to the attacking fleet, proving that Yarnell had been more than just lucky. Still, as late as the spring of 1941 the US Navy view remained that 'the

power of aviation is increasing,' but 'the strength of the battle line is still the decisive factor.'

To defend against surprise carrier attack the United States had great hopes for the Boeing B-17 Flying Fortress, first flown in 1935. The B-17 was planned as an anti-shipping weapon to strike at long range from the American coast or from Oahu against an approaching enemy fleet, very much as Billy Mitchell had argued in the 1920s. One year after the B-17 appeared the Japanese, at Yamamoto's original suggestion, produced the Mitsubishi G3M3 Type 96 'Nell,' at the time the fastest land-based bomber in the world. (American practice was to name Japanese bombers after women and fighters after men. The one exception was the outstanding Japanese carrier fighter, the Mitsubishi A6M2 'Zero,' which also first appeared in 1935, and for which the American name of 'Zeke' never became popular.) The existence of these land-based bombers made the possession by either side of small islands in the Pacific and South Seas of crucial military importance.

In 1933 the Japanese Imperial Navy faced a purge by Navy Minister Osumi Mineo, a member of the Fleet school, in which members of the moderate faction were retired or steered into positions of no importance. One of the few survivors

was Vice-Admiral Yamamoto, who in October 1934 was sent to tell a preliminary conference on naval matters in London that Japan intended to terminate its previous naval treaties. The situation was such that any leader who opposed the Imperial Navy in this would probably have faced assassination. Yamamoto continued to thrive partly through caution and competence, and partly because his unusual belief in aircraft placed him to one side of the main naval debates. In 1936 he was appointed Director of the Imperial Navy's Air Department.

At the Second London Naval Conference, beginning on 6 January 1936, the Japanese delegation announced that they would accept nothing but parity in warships with the United States and Great Britain. When this was inevitably refused, the Japanese withdrew from the conference on 15 January, leaving the United States, France, Britain and its major dominions to agree a treaty among themselves on 25 March. After a year the Fleet school set in motion the 'third supplemental building program,' for which it had planned since 1934. This meant the modernization of all Japanese battleships and battle-cruisers, including the *Nagato*. It also meant the building of two entirely new super-battleships, *Yamato* and *Musashi*, each of 70,000 tons carrying nine 18.2-inch guns. The Fleet school placed its faith in extremely accurate rapid shooting from these monsters, which would outrange anything else afloat.

On 26 February 1936 another attempted military coup, a full-scale mutiny far more serious than anything which had gone before, took place in

Tokyo. Involving at least 1400 soldiers, it resulted in the deaths of Prime Minister Okada Keisuke and three other serving or former ministers before order could be restored, partly with the Navy's help. This, at least, was too large an event to ignore, and most of the ringleaders were executed.

Against this background the Japanese Army and Navy at last reached a deal. Since 1935 the Army, although intent on its advance into China, had been aware of the growing threat from the Soviet Union, which had three times as many men in the Far East as the Japanese. The Kwantung Army, now spread throughout Manchukuo, did not consider itself capable of war with the Soviet Union until 1940, and for the intervening years the Army was prepared to go along with the Navy's plans for expansion southward, toward the oil, rubber, and other natural resources held by the British, French and Dutch empires in South East

Asia. In return the Navy agreed to the creation of 10 new divisions for the Army, plus more aircraft. This new policy was put forward by the two services on 11 May, and agreed by the five ministers on 7 August. For the first time, it listed Great Britain among Japan's probable enemies, and the principal aim of the Navy as 'building up forces to maintain an ascendancy in the Western Pacific against the American fleet.' On 25 November 1936 Japan and Germany signed the Anti-Comintern Pact, an agreement aimed at blocking the ambitions of the Soviet Union.

The British government had in 1934 decided to fortify Singapore as a major naval base, in case of a Japanese move southward. Great Britain, however, was increasingly preoccupied with the likelihood of war in Europe against Germany. If that happened, ships might be spared for Singapore to challenge the Japanese, but not troops. The British were well

ABOVE LEFT: One of the outstanding carrier fighters of World War II, a Mitsubishi A6M2 or A6M3 'Zero' of the Japanese Imperial Navy.

ABOVE: The massive *Yamato*, new flagship of the Japanese Imperial Navy, shortly after its launch in 1940.

LEFT: The Japanese flagship *Nagato* shown before its modernization in 1936.

RIGHT: Japanese troops and tanks of the Kwantung Army shown in Manchuria before the attack on China itself.

aware that Japan, to reach Malaya or Borneo, must first deal with the Philippines. In 1935 the Americans announced that the islands would be given independence before 1946, but this did not affect the pledge to defend them. Even without a formal agreement, the British had little choice after about 1937 but to leave their interests in the Far East to the United States. Equally, the United States had little choice but to accept the responsibility, if it wished to avoid Japanese domination of the area.

On 4 June 1937, after the usual disagreement between the Japanese Army and Navy, both accepted Prince Konoe Fumimaro, the elderly leader of the House of Peers, as Prime Minister. With Konoe as a figurehead, the five ministers plus the two chiefs of staff then agreed legislation in the Emperor's name placing civil aviation and fuel supplies under government control, creating an Imperial Headquarters in the hope of at least coordinating Army and Navy policy, and assembling a planning board to control the Japanese economy, the beginnings of industrial mobilization for war. On 7 July 1937, on the flimsiest of pretexts after a shooting incident at the Marco Polo Bridge (modern Lukouchiao) near Peking, the Kwantung Army plunged Japan into that war with an all-out attack on Nationalist China. It remained to be seen how the United States would react.

CHAPTER THREE

THE PLANS
FOR WAR

FOR THE Chinese Nationalists the war with Japan, which the Japanese themselves never called anything but 'The China Incident,' was hardly unexpected. But in 1937 there was little that Chiang Kai-shek could do to stop the Japanese, even after forming a United Front with the Chinese Communists under Mao Tse-tung in September. Peking (known at the time, with some irony, as *Peiping* or 'Northern Peace') fell to the Japanese on 28 July and Tientsin a day later. By the end of August the main Chinese trading ports were all under siege. Although Chinese resistance gradually strengthened, Shanghai fell to the Japanese on 8 November with heavy losses, and on 13 December Japanese forces at last fought their way through to the Nationalist capital of Nanking.

What followed became known as 'the rape of Nanking,' a six-week systematic looting and destruction of the city by the Japanese in which at least 200,000 Chinese were killed. The shock of the massacre went round the world as Japanese troops proudly allowed Western journalists and newsreel teams to record their achievement. Elsewhere, Japanese soldiers were reported as weeping with shame at the disgrace. To underline the Japanese government's lack of control over its own forces, on 12 December near Nanking Japanese shore batteries and carrier aircraft attacked and sank the gunboat USS *Panay*, killing some of the crew. Only a prompt

Japanese apology and payment of $2 million in compensation prevented a major crisis. 'Never before,' noted the American ambassador in Tokyo, Joseph Grew, 'has the fact that there are "two Japans" been more clearly emphasized'.

Refusing to negotiate with the Japanese, Chiang Kai-shek fought on, moving his capital first to Hankow (part of modern Wuhan), and then on 25 October 1938 to the inaccessible city of Chungking in western China, protected by the gorges of the Yangtze River. From there the Nationalists had three safe supply lines: to French Indochina (modern Vietnam), to British-owned Burma, and over the old Silk Road to Mongolia and the Soviet Union. Otherwise, by the end of 1938, the Japanese held virtually the whole of northern and eastern China, including the coal and iron ore mining regions, and every major city except for Chungking and Hong Kong.

The Japanese Army had won a great military victory, and by its own standards a degree of military glory. What it had not won was a source of economic prosperity for Japan. On the contrary, China had turned into a terrible trap for the Japanese. To support the occupation force of 1,500,000 troops was costing Japan at least $5 million a day. In December 1937 the 'Spiritual Mobilization Central League' was set up as an arm of the cabinet to boost the Japanese people's resolve for the difficult times

PREVIOUS PAGES: Shanghai under Japanese bombardment, 1937.

BELOW LEFT: Japanese troops entering Nanking in 1937.

RIGHT: Crew members of USS *Panay* returning the fire of Japanese aircraft in an unsuccessful attempt to prevent their ship being sunk.

RIGHT: The execution of Chinese civilians by Japanese soldiers during the 'Rape of Nanking.'

*Prime Minister Konoe explained that the
Japanese objective in China was the creation
of a 'New Order in East Asia.'*

LEFT: Japanese soldiers celebrating their victory with a salute of *'Banzai'* for their emperor.

BELOW: Emperor Hirohito (center) with Prime Minister Prince Konoe Fumimaro (on the emperor's left) and his first cabinet in 1937. The Army and Navy ministers are standing next to the emperor.

ahead, and on 1 April 1938 Japan introduced the National General Mobilization Law, placing the country on a full war footing including rationing and state control of industry.

On 22 December 1938 Prime Minister Konoe, in an official statement, explained the Japanese objective in China as the creation of a 'New Order in East Asia.' Japan wanted no Chinese territory, requiring only 'the minimum guarantee necessary for the execution by China of her function as a participant in the establishment of the new order.' Konoe was quite sincere. As the only semi-divine race on earth the Japanese expected the Chinese to contribute willingly to their country's domination by the forces of the Emperor.

Always inclined to see foreign policy in moral terms, the United States made no secret of its indignation at Japanese behavior in China. 'When an epidemic of physical disease starts to spread,' President Roosevelt told a Chicago audience on 5 October 1937, 'the community

approves and joins in a quarantine of the patients.' He promptly canceled the 1911 trade agreement with Japan. On 6 November 1937 the Japanese agreed with the Germans to admit Italy to the Anti-Comintern Pact, completing the Berlin-Rome-Tokyo Axis and linking Japan firmly to Adolf Hitler's Germany, viewed by most Americans as the principal threat to world peace. For the first time the American government faced a probable two-front war against Japan and Germany, just as Theodore Roosevelt had once feared.

As a result, in 1938 the United States drew up its 'Rainbow' plans for a possible world war. To take the offensive both against Germany and Japan, the US Navy argued, would need a fleet three times the size of that available. Even to control the Atlantic would require a doubling of the existing fleet to 27 battleships, 12 carriers and nearly 300 smaller ships. Admiral Yarnell therefore proposed the plan finally adopted as Rainbow Two. Making no attempt to force a

decisive battle in the Pacific, the United States would rely on a long-range economic blcokade of Japan, using aircraft, fast carrier groups and submarines to harrass and sink Japanese merchant shipping, gaining time until the Navy was strong enough to take the offensive in the Pacific.

This plan made a great deal of sense. In 1938, the United States took 40 percent of Japan's exports and supplied over half its imports, including two-thirds of its oil imports (virtually all the remainder coming from the Dutch East Indies and British Borneo). Lacking iron ore, Japan also imported more than 2.5 million tons of scrap iron each year from the United States. Forty percent of all goods entering or leaving Japan were carried in foreign merchant vessels. With a population now greater than 70 million, the Japanese home islands could not even clothe and feed themselves any longer. In short, Japan was frighteningly vulnerable to blockade. What was more, Roosevelt liked Yarnell's plan. 'It goes along with that word "quarantine" I used in Chicago last month,' he observed.

On 10 February 1939, in a continued effort to defeat the Chinese Nationalists while at the same time pressing southward, Japanese forces occupied Hainan Island, dominating the Gulf of Tonkin. On 31 March they added Spratley Island, which, lying west of the Philippines, was uninhabited but claimed by France. On 6 March the 'fourth supplemental building program' was begun, adding another two battleships, a carrier and 30 smaller ships to the fleet. Not until this program was completed, the Imperial Navy believed, could it safely face war with the United States. At the same time, the Army was testing British resolve with the 'Tientsin Crisis,' a series of petty harrassments aimed at the British concession area of Tientsin.

The Soviet Union remained a problem for Japan. It could hardly afford war with China, Russia, Great Britain and the United States at the same time. But neither would the Kwantung Army permit Soviet support of the *Kuomintang*, or give in to Soviet pressure. In June 1938 came the 'Changkufeng Incident' (modern Chokoho), a squabble on the frontier between Manchukuo, Korea and Soviet Siberia which, after some serious fighting, died down after two months. It was followed within a year by the 'Nomonhan Incident,' an undeclared war on the border between Manchukuo and Soviet-controlled Mongolia which ended in a major defeat and over 20,000 casual-

ties for the Kwantung Army.

Even as the last battle of this war was being fought, the Soviet Union announced its signing of a Friendship Pact with Germany on 23 August 1939. This remarkable betrayal by the Germans of the Anti-Comintern Pact led the Japanese to conclude their own armistice with the Soviet Union on 16 September. Both sides, intent on threats from another direction, had learned that it was safer to leave each other alone. After more than a year of cautious negotiation, on 13 April 1941 they reached the Soviet-Japanese Neutrality Pact, agreeing not to attack each other and to stand neutral in each other's wars. The Silk Road supply route to the Chinese Nationalists was closed.

Meanwhile, to the disappointment of Ambassador Grew in Tokyo, Admiral Yamamoto, who had risen steadily to the

BELOW: Japanese soldiers with a Soviet prisoner during the 'Nomonhan Incident' in 1939.

RIGHT: Swordfish torpedo bombers of the Fleet Air Arm taking off from the deck of HMS *Illustrious* in the Mediterranean, 1941.

post of Vice-Minister of the Navy, was not appointed as Minister. Instead, on 30 August 1939, Yamamoto was promoted to Commander-in-Chief of the Combined Fleet. Although the Imperial Navy's highest honor, this meant that Yamamoto could no longer influence naval policy – or so it seemed.

Then, on the far side of the world, on 1 September 1939 Adolf Hitler's Germany invaded Poland, and two days later found itself at war with Britain and France. For a few months this European war almost seemed to bring peace to the Far East, as the attention of the Western powers turned away from Japan. The big change came on 10 May 1940, when German forces attacked and overran France, Belgium and the Netherlands in three weeks, leaving their Far East possessions without protection. France even signed an armistice with Germany on 22 July, putting French colonies under the control of a virtually powerless new French republic, with its capital at Vichy. On 10 June Italy also declared war against Great Britain. The British, who had relied on the French Fleet to cover the Western Mediterranean for them, were instead forced to sink it themselves at Oran, rather than risk its falling into German hands. This new commitment left them virtually nothing with which to defend the Far East.

The fall of France also galvanized the Americans into a massive rearmament program, aimed chiefly at Germany. Although neutral, the United States' behavior was hardly impartial. President Roosevelt lacked the political support to declare outright war on Germany, but was unwilling to see Britain defeated. After a decade of underspending, Congress authorized in June and July 1940 a total of $5 billion to create what Roosevelt would later call 'the arsenal of democracy,' and on 16 July the President signed the Two Ocean Expansion Act for the Navy. The effect of this on Japanese plans was devastating. By the end of 1941, Japan would have in the Pacific 10 capital ships, 10 aircraft carriers, 38 cruisers, 112 destroyers and 65 submarines, compared to an American fleet of eight capital ships, three carriers, 24 cruisers, 80 destroyers and 56 submarines. But the United States would at the same time be *building* 15 capital ships, 11 carriers, 54 cruisers, 191 destroyers and 73 submarines, or more than the entire Japanese Combined Fleet. The ratio of forces between the US Navy and the Imperial Navy would be 10:7 in late 1941, but 10:3 by 1944. This was the

measure of American economic and industrial superiority over Japan.

As a mark of the turbulence of Japanese politics, there were no fewer than four changes of government between January 1939 and July 1940, although policy remained a matter of agreement between the Army and Navy. Indeed, the cabinet which formed on 22 July 1940 was headed once more by Prince Konoe. On 4 July the Japanese Army finally backed completely the Navy's strategy of expansion southward, while holding on the defensive against the Soviet Union. Taking advantage of the impossible situation faced by the new British Prime Minister, Winston Churchill, the Japanese pressured him into closing the Burma Road through to the Chinese Nationalists at Chungking on 27 July. The final supply route, through Haiphong in French Indochina, was closed by an agreement forced upon the Vichy French government on 26 July, which permitted the stationing of Japanese troops in northern Indochina. On 27 September, Japan together with Germany and Italy signed the Tripartite Pact in Berlin, calling for each country to

assist the others if they were attacked by a country not then involved either in the European War or in the China Incident, specifically excluding the Soviet Union. Since it could apply to no other major power, it was hard for the American government to interpret this Pact as anything other than a direct threat to the United States.

In response to the Japanese arrival in French Indochina the United States resorted to economic sanctions. President Roosevelt imposed an embargo on the export of aviation fuel to Japan on 1 August, extending it to include scrap iron in September and all iron and steel in December, following his re-election as President. Meanwhile, with American support, the British reopened the Burma Road in October. On 11 November the British also gave a smart little demonstration of aircraft carrier effectiveness, when 21 Swordfish torpedo bombers from HMS *Illustrious* carried out an attack on the Italian fleet, apparently safe behind its torpedo nets in the shallow harbor of Taranto. Half the main Italian force, three battleships, a cruiser and two destroyers, was badly damaged in the attack

puzzled that their superiors seemed to know more than they were telling. Even the Navy's Combat Intelligence Unit at Pearl Harbor under Commander Joseph Rochefort, which was reading about 10 percent of Japanese military and naval codes, knew nothing about Magic.

The Japanese were also reading some American codes, but in the last days of 1940 sheer good luck gave them one of the most important Intelligence breaks of the war. A British merchant ship, SS *Automedon*, was intercepted near Sumatra by a German surface raider while carrying a top secret report for the British Commander-in-Chief Far East. On 12 December the Germans passed the report to the Japanese. It showed that there was no combined plan between the British and Americans for the defense of the Far East, that the defenses of Singapore were weak, and that there would be virtually no British reinforcements arriving. By 18 December, Admiral Yamamoto had come to a decision: the Southern Operation would go ahead, and it would include a surprise carrier strike against the American Pacific Fleet at Pearl Harbor.

Yamamoto's logic was inescapable. The American Two-Ocean Navy meant that Japan had at most a year in which to establish its position in the Far East. To win the war in China, or even to survive as a nation, Japan needed the economic resources of the British and Dutch Empires. To reach those resources, it was impossible to by-pass the Philippines. So, there would be war with Great Britain, the Netherlands, and the United States. In order to allow Japan a free hand, the US Pacific Fleet had to be knocked out for at least six months. For Yamamoto the attack on Pearl Harbor was a vital *defensive* move to secure the open Pacific flank of the new Japanese Empire.

The full Southern Operation, which would take months of planning to finalize, was a remarkable feat of arms founded on very slender resources. So great were the demands of China that, of Japan's 51 divisions, only 11 could be spared to conquer nine separate countries. The first phase, including Pearl Harbor, would be a surprise assault coordinated over seven time zones from Hawaii to Malaya, in which Thailand, northern Malaya (modern Malaysia), the island of Borneo and the Philippines would be attacked together. At the same time, Japanese forces would capture Guam, Wake and the Gilbert Islands (modern Tuvalu) out in the Pacific. Together with the islands

which altered the balance of naval forces in the Mediterranean overnight. The Japanese naval attaché in London, Lieutenant-Commander Genda Minoru, made a special study of the raid.

On 25 September 1940, United States Intelligence scored a major victory by breaking the chief Japanese diplomatic code, known as Code Purple, by a system which they called 'Magic.' By the time that the new Japanese ambassador to Washington, Admiral Nomura Kichisaburo, presented his credentials to Secretary of State Cordell Hull in Washington on 12 February 1941, the State Depart-

ment was reading the traffic between Tokyo and the Japanese Embassy on a regular basis. Even so, Magic had its drawbacks, as messages could take days to decypher, translate, and interpret. More importantly, it was not realized that Ambassador Nomura, who was sent to look for peace with the United States, was not always fully briefed on his own government's policies. Further, so afraid were the Americans of their secret leaking out that the circulation of Magic was very small, for a time not even including the President. For the next year, US Army and Navy commanders would be

LEFT: Italian battleships beached in Taranto harbor following the British raid.

BELOW: Admiral Nomura Kichisaburo, the new Japanese Ambassador to Washington, meeting Secretary of State Cordell Hull in February 1941.

already held by the Japanese, these would form the 'Line of the Rising Sun,' a defensive barrier against the Americans. In the second phase, the rest of Malaya and Singapore, together with southern Burma, would be occupied. Finally, the third phase would take in northern Burma, together with Java, Sumatra and the other islands of the Dutch East Indies, producing an economically self-sufficient and defensible Empire, the 'Greater Asia Co-Prosperity Sphere.' To accomplish this the Japanese allowed themselves just under six months before facing the American response.

It was clear that Japan could not defeat the United States in a long war. Japanese assessments placed American war-making potential as about 10 times that of Japan. Even with the Co-Prosperity Sphere established, the demands of war with the United States would cause the Empire to run out of oil within two to three years. In September 1941 the Imperial Navy's Chief of Staff told the cabinet: 'We can successfully oppose the United States in war for a period of two years. Any longer conflict would tend to be unprofitable for Japan.'

Yamamoto's own estimate was

*By July 1941, Tokyo had a detailed
picture of the US Pacific Fleet's ships at
Pearl Harbor and their movements.*

slightly less optimistic. 'If I am told to fight regardless of the consequences,' he told Prince Konoe in 1940, 'I shall run completely wild for the first six months or a year, but I have no confidence at all in the second and third years.' The main Japanese hope was that they expected to win the great naval encounter when it came, sinking the American Pacific Fleet, and to inflict heavy casualties on the Americans as they tried to break through the Line of the Rising Sun. Meanwhile, Germany would surely defeat Britain and win the European war. The United States, lacking Samurai spirit and the determination bred of Japanese cultural superiority, would then perhaps give up and leave Japan in peace.

Yamamoto himself never shared this reading of the American character. 'To make victory certain,' he wrote in January 1941, 'we would have to march into Washington and dictate the terms of peace in the White House.' But since the Meiji Restoration the Japanese had faced and overcome impossible odds to extend the Emperor's rule. It was unthinkable that they should give up in the face of the ultimate test. Yamamoto therefore devised, and forced through against the opposition of the Navy Staff, an attack plan for a war which he was personally convinced that Japan would lose. 'What a strange position I find myself in,' he wrote on 11 November 1941, 'having to pursue with full determination a course of action which is diametrically opposed to my best judgment and firmest conviction. That, too, perhaps is *karma*.'

On 1 February 1941 a new Commander-in-Chief Pacific was appointed at Pearl Harbor, Admiral Husband E Kimmel, an outstanding officer who had been promoted from Rear Admiral over the heads of a number of his seniors. (Kimmel was also promoted Commander-in-Chief of the US Fleet, by 1941 largely an honorary title.) Three days later, Lieutenant-General Walter C Short was appointed Commander-in-Chief of the US Army's Hawaiian Department. Both men faced the problems and attitudes typical of peacetime armed forces, above all a shortage of equipment. Kimmel saw his main task as training the Pacific Fleet for the coming war. His ships left harbor every Monday or Tuesday for exercises at sea, returning on Friday to give the sailors a rest. For the one or two Japanese naval officers operating as spies from the consulate in Honolulu keeping track of the Fleet could hardly have been easier,

since its anchorage lay in full view of the surrounding countryside, and by July 1941 Tokyo had a detailed picture of the ships and their movements.

Lieutenant-General Short also believed in thorough training for his troops. But there was an important gap in his thinking, revealed by a major Army exercise on 12 May 1941, in which a notional enemy carrier force approaching from the north – as in 1932 – was detected and attacked by the 21 B-17s then based on Oahu, following which Short's ground forces repulsed an attempted amphibious landing. Short's plan did not include the protection of Kimmel's ships, which he assumed to be at sea. He was also not 'air minded,' regarding the land battle as his principal task. In fact, Short was far more concerned about possible sabotage to his aircraft from Japanese living in the Hawaiian Islands than about the threat of air attack.

Yamamoto, meanwhile, had given the planning of 'Operation Hawaii' to the

ABOVE LEFT: Commander Genda Minoru in old age.

LEFT, FROM TOP TO BOTTOM: The *Kaga*, the *Shokaku* and the *Soryu*.

TOP: The *Akagi*, flagship of the First Air Fleet.

ABOVE: The *Zuikaku*, newest of the Japanese carriers and sister ship to the *Shokaku*. The remaining carrier of First Air Fleet, the *Hiryu*, was a sister ship to the *Soryu*.

brilliant Commander Genda Minoru, now back from London as air operations officer for the Imperial Navy's 1st Carrier Division. After some deliberation, Genda concluded that the principal target for an airstrike must be the Pacific Fleet, with priority given to the carriers, then the battleships. To make the blow as heavy as possible Genda asked for an entirely new formation, the *Kido Butai* or First Air Fleet, consisting of 1st Carrier Division (*Akagi* and *Kaga*), 2nd Carrier Division (the light carriers *Soryu* and *Hiryu*), and when it became available in September 5th Carrier Division (the two most recent Japanese carriers, *Zuikaku* and *Shokaku*).

LEFT: Vice Admiral Nagumo Chuichi at about the time of Pearl Harbor.

ABOVE: Commander Fuchida Mitsuo, taken in old age.

First Air Fleet came into existence on 10 April, commanded by Vice Admiral Nagumo Chuichi, a torpedo specialist rather than an airman, who had deep misgivings about the plan. From May onward, Commander Fuchida Mitsuo, who would himself lead the Pearl Harbor airstrike, practised with his pilots to solve the technical problems of shallow water torpedo runs and of successful mid-altitude bombing and dive-bombing of ships. By 29 July the basic planning was completed. To win over the more ortho-dox members of the Navy Staff, Yama-moto also agreed to a simultaneous sub-marine attack on the Pacific Fleet, including miniature submarines which would penetrate Pearl Harbor itself. This part of the operation was given to Vice Admiral Shimizu Mitsumi.

Even while remaining neutral, the United States continued to do everything in its power to aid the British. On 11 March the Lend-Lease agreement was signed, in effect giving Britain unlimited access to American weapons and muni-tions, and American help was promised for convoy escorts in the Atlantic. On 24 April Admiral Kimmel was told to give up the carrier *Yorktown* and three of his battleships to the Atlantic Fleet. By the middle of July a quarter of his fighting ships had been sent to the Atlantic, and with them so many support ships and oilers that the Pacific Fleet could not have reached the Philippines without running out of fuel.

Then, an event on the far side of the world from Japan once again trans-formed the situation in the Pacific. On 22 June 1941 Germany together with its European allies launched an unprovoked attack upon the Soviet Union. With Russia distracted, Japan now had nothing to fear in Manchuria. On 2 July a rare Imperial Conference of senior Japanese ministers agreed that, while every effort should be made to preserve peace, in order to get what it wanted 'Japan shall not decline war with Britain and the United States.' On 21 July, after the formality of an agreement with the Vichy government, Japanese troops quickly occupied the remainder of French Indochina.

The United States' response was to freeze all Japanese (and Chinese) assets in America on 26 July, proposing that the Japanese withdraw and declare Indo-china a neutral country. Almost by way of reply, on 30 July a flight of Japanese aircraft tried to bomb the gunboat USS *Tutuila* at Chungking. The Japanese apologized, but stayed in Indochina. As a result, on 1 August the United States im-posed an embargo of crude oil and high octane fuel on Japan. This was followed by the Atlantic Charter Declaration of 12 August 1941, jointly with the British, which stressed the importance of respect for other nations' territory, and came perilously close to looking like a formal alliance.

In the early spring of 1941, at about the same time that Yamamoto began the Pearl Harbor plan, the United States started to update Rainbow Two. The finished plan, Rainbow Five, was adopted on 14 May. Its basic strategy re-mained the same: to defeat Germany and Italy in Europe while remaining on the defensive in the Pacific. It was now accepted that the Philippines could not be held, and whatever defenses could be mounted for the Far East must be largely left to the British. The Pacific Fleet's role was to keep its own communications with the United States open, while car-riers and submarines, as before, carried out raids on the Japanese.

Then, following the Japanese occupa-tion of French Indochina, came an im-portant change. The former US Army Chief of Staff, General Douglas Mac-Arthur, had been sent out to the Philip-pines in 1935 to organize the islands' defenses. MacArthur argued that, if given enough weapons and equipment before war broke out, the Philippines could be held against the Japanese. On 26 July Roosevelt agreed to this, and by 1 August the first shipments of tanks, guns and aircraft were on their way to Mac-Arthur, including by the end of Novem-ber 35 of the crucially important B-17s. These aircraft were badly needed else-where, and nowhere more than at Pearl Harbor where the number available had actually been reduced to 12 by Mac-Arthur's demands.

On 4 September the Japanese cabinet met to approve its 'minimum demands' and 'maximum concessions' in the face of the American oil embargo, allowing its diplomats until 15 October to reach a peaceful settlement, after which prepa-rations for war would begin. The mini-mum demands included no outside inter-ference in the China Incident, the closing of the Burma Road, and the Western abandonment of Chiang Kai-shek. The maximum concessions included the pos-sible negotiated reduction of Japanese troops in China, a promise not to use Indochina as a base for operations except against China, and a guarantee of the neutrality of the Philippines should the United States enter the European war.

*By 8 October, the date and time for the
attack on Pearl Harbor had been agreed:
0800 hours on Sunday 7 December.*

As Ambassador Nomura was well aware, this was no basis for agreement with the United States. The decision was important enough to require a further Imperial Conference on 6 September, at which, astonishingly and against all precedent, the Emperor himself spoke, reading aloud a poem written by the Emperor Meiji – 'The seas of the world are all brothers, then why do the waves and the winds clash and rage?' In so far as he could, Hirohito the Showa Emperor had cast his vote for peace.

Between 11 and 20 September a series of wargames was carried out at the Japanese Naval War College to test Operation Hawaii. The attack would be launched from about 250 miles north of the Hawaiian Islands, well within American reconnaissance and bomber range. On his first attempt, Nagumo's fleet was detected, his aircraft were intercepted over the target, and he retired having lost two carriers for little gain. On the second attempt the carriers planned their attack to start at dawn, and this time achieved surprise. The choice fell naturally on a Sunday morning, when the Pacific Fleet would almost certainly be in harbor. By 8 October the date and time for the attack had been agreed at 0800 hours on Sunday 7 December.

The threat of war between the United States and Japan was now obvious to any American who could read a newspaper. At the same time, the idea of Japan going to war with the United States seemed incredible, and that a Japanese carrier fleet would attack Pearl Harbor more incredible still. On 24 September the Japanese consulate in Honolulu received orders from Tokyo to plot exactly, by means of an imaginary grid, the positions of all ships in Pearl Harbor. Although this message was broken by Magic, it was not passed to either Admiral Kimmel or Lieutenant-General Short, nor did anyone reach the obvious conclusion about its purpose. At no time before the attack did either man receive a specific warning of a threat to Pearl Harbor.

On 16 October, the day after the deadline for a negotiated peace had passed, Prince Konoe resigned and was replaced as Prime Minister by his former Army Minister, General Tojo Hideki, regarded by all as an aggressive politician with little thought for peace. At once, Ambassador Nomura offered his resignation. It was refused, and for the next two months he found himself in the impossible position of negotiating without the trust of

his own government. Facing war as Prime Minister, however, General Tojo had a sudden attack of nerves, not helped by the fact that, under the Japanese system, the Navy would not tell him the date on which the Southern Operation was due to start. The Imperial Navy Staff also had a similar attack of nerves on 18 October, reducing the planned strike at Pearl Harbor from six carriers to three. Yamamoto promptly threatened to resign, and the three carriers were reinstated in the plan.

On 5 November a final Imperial Conference agreed to try again with new proposals for the Americans, but to continue the preparations for war. As the alert went out, Japanese merchant vessels round the world started to head for their home ports – a fact noted by British and American Intelligence. On 11 November the first Japanese submarines left their

home waters in order to be in position blockading ports on the west coast of the United States by 4 December. On 17 November Yamamoto addressed the officers aboard the *Akagi*. 'It is the code of *bushido* to select an equal or stronger opponent,' he observed. 'On this score you have nothing to complain about – the United States Navy is a good match for the Japanese Navy.' That evening, Admiral Nagumo's First Air Fleet began to leave Saeki Bay for its first rendezvous in the Kurile Islands. Three days later, the invasion force destined for Malaya left harbor, followed on 29 November by the invasion force for Guam.

By this date, although Hull and Nomura continued to work hard for an understanding that both knew did not exist, Roosevelt's government was convinced that there was going to be a war. 'The Japs are notorious for making an attack without warning,' noted Secretary for War Henry Stimson on 25 November. 'The question was how we should maneuver them into firing the first shot

without allowing too much danger to ourselves.' Next day, Secretary Hull rejected Nomura's last proposals, which would have left China and Indochina both in Japanese hands. In the next 24 hours both the Army and Navy sent general alerts to their senior commanders that war was imminent. 'Prior to hostile Japanese action,' read the message received by Lieutenant-General Short on 27 November, 'you are directed to undertake such reconnaissance and other measures as you deem necessary.' Admiral Kimmel's instructions were even more strongly phrased, opening: 'This despatch is to be considered a war warning.' Again, neither mentioned Pearl Harbor as a specific target, and left both men confused as to their precise orders.

On the same day, 27 November, the Japanese Navy Minister informed Prime Minister Tojo of the date of the Pearl Harbor attack, and he in turn pressed Ambassador Nomura to keep negotiations open for another two days. On 30 November, the Japanese Ambassador in Berlin met with the German Foreign Minister, Joachim von Ribbentrop, who advised him that: 'Should Japan become engaged in a war against the United States, Germany, of course, would enter the war immediately.' On 3 December Japanese embassies and consulates around the world were ordered to destroy all secret documents and codes. Broken by Magic, this message was actually passed to Admiral Kimmel against security regulations. US Naval Intelligence, both in Washington and at Pearl Harbor, had already begun to build up a picture of the Japanese convoys heading for Malaya and Guam. Commander Rochefort's codebreakers were also tracking the Japanese submarines toward the Hawaiian Islands.

On 4 December it was agreed in Tokyo that the final communication with the American government should be transmitted on 6 December for delivery to Secretary Hull by Ambassador Nomura at 1330 hours on 7 December, equivalent to 0300 hours on 8 December in Tokyo or 0730 hours on 7 December in the Hawaiian Islands, where the attack would take place at 0800 hours. As soon as transmission began on the morning of 6 December, the American Magic codebreakers began to read the message. At about 2100 hours a copy lacking only the last section was delivered to Roosevelt's office in the White House. The President read it through. 'This means war,' he said.

LEFT: Douglas MacArthur, shown after his promotion to General of the Army in 1945.

RIGHT: The cabinet of Prime Minister Tojo Hideki on its formation in October 1941.

RIGHT: General Tojo Hideki shortly after becoming Prime Minister of Japan.

CHAPTER FOUR

OAHU UNDER ATTACK

AT 0600 hours on 26 November Tokyo time, Admiral Nagumo's First Air Fleet left its anchorage at Hitokappu Bay in the Kurile Islands. Nagumo's chief problem, and one of the many reasons the Americans believed a Japanese attack on Pearl Harbor was impossible, was making the round trip of some 9000 nautical miles without running out of fuel. The *Akagi* and *Kaga* just about had this kind of range, as did the brand new *Shokaku* and *Zuikaku*, but not the smaller *Hiryu* and *Soryu*, nor the heavy escort cruisers *Tone* and *Chikuma*. The fuel problem, together with Imperial Navy doctrine and Nagumo's own traditional views, meant that he took with his carriers and cruisers the battleships *Kirishima* and *Hiei*, a squadron of nine destroyers led by the light cruiser *Abukuma*, two more destroyers to bombard Midway Island as a diversion, eight oilers in two supply groups, and three long-range submarines, altogether 33 vessels steaming at no better than 14 knots. The fuel situation was not critical, but there was not much of a reserve should the carriers have to maneuver or run at high speed. For a force this large to get half-way across the Pacific undetected would need good planning and a great deal of luck. Nagumo's orders were to turn back if spotted before the day of the attack.

The plan called for First Air Fleet to steam due east along the 43rd Parallel, an area of the Pacific usually free of commercial vessels and fishing fleets, reaching a point roughly 2000 miles north of the Hawaiian Islands by 3 December (local time – despite crossing the International Date Line, First Air Fleet kept to Tokyo time throughout its mission). A course change southeast would then take Nagumo to his second turning point, about 700 miles due north of the Hawaiian Islands, by 6 December. There the carriers would start their run southward through the night, coming well within range of American long-range scouting aircraft by dawn. If all went well, then about 250 miles north of Oahu, at one hour before sunrise, 0600 hours on 7 December (0130 hours on 8 December in Tokyo), the first wave of aircraft would launch.

In the three days before sailing, Commanders Genda and Fuchida worked to make sure that everyone understood their plan. The target of the attack was the US Pacific Fleet, above all its carriers and battleships. How many carriers they would find was uncertain – at least two, possbily three or even four. By the morn-

ing of the attack First Air Fleet would know, by messages from the Honolulu consulate and from Japanese submarines lying off the Hawaiian Islands, whether or not the Americans were in Pearl Harbor as usual on a Sunday. Ideally, Admiral Kimmel would have moved his ships for 'safety' to Lahina Roads, off Maui Island, where they could be sunk in deep water. If they were at sea, they would be hunted and engaged.

If the Pacific Fleet was, as expected, at Pearl Harbor, Fuchida would lead an attack force of two waves against it. The crews of the *Shokaku* and *Zuikaku*, on their first voyage, were thought too inexperienced to tackle the main objective. All their aircraft, plus the fighters from the other carriers, were to attack the US Army Air Force bases on Oahu, the US Navy air base on Ford Island in the middle of Pearl Harbor and the Marine Corps base at nearby Ewa Bay, hoping to catch the enemy aircraft on the ground. The first wave would be 45 Mitsubishi A6M2 'Zero' fighters, 89 Nakajima B5N2 'Kate' bombers and 51 Aichi D3A2 'Val' dive-bombers. The Vals, each carrying one 250 kilogram bomb, were to attack the airfields together with the Zeros. Meanwhile 49 Kates, each carrying a single 800 kilogram bomb made by adapting a 16-inch naval shell, would bomb the Pacific Fleet from about 10,000 feet. The remainder, each carrying a single torpedo, would make low-level runs across the anchorage. Genda and Fuchida concealed from Admiral Nagumo an agreement between the pilots that, if the torpedos could not penetrate the American torpedo nets, aircraft would crash into them in a suicide

PREVIOUS PAGES: The magazines of the destroyer USS *Shaw* explode during the Japanese attack on Pearl Harbor.

RIGHT: The aircraft that attacked Pearl Harbor. Top to bottom: a Nakajima B5N2 'Kate' light bomber; a Mitsubishi A6M2 'Zero' fighter; and an Achi D3A2 'Val' dive bomber, all of the Japanese Imperial Navy.

BELOW: The battleship *Kirishima*, one of the two battleships of the support group for First Air Fleet.

attempt to clear the way.

By the time the second wave arrived, half an hour after the first, it was expected that surprise would be lost, and no low-level torpedo bombers were included. This wave, which would concentrate on any unsunk carriers or battleships, would be made up of 54 Kates from the *Shokaku* and *Zuikaku*, 36 Vals and 44 Zeros (equipped as fighter-bombers) from the other carriers, and 36 Zero fighters as protection. Altogether, 355 aircraft would take part in the strike, leaving 80 fighters in reserve to protect the carriers.

Genda and Fuchida both argued for the plan to include further strikes after the first, particularly if the American carriers were at sea and had to be hunted down. Although not rejecting this idea outright, Nagumo remained privately opposed to it. From his experience of the wargames in September he expected to lose at least two carriers in the attack, and Japanese planning margins for the Southern Operation were already impossibly tight. Nagumo considered Genda's plan to be quite risky enough as it was.

The submarine attack was left as a separate operation, which would succeed or fail independently of the air attack. If the Pacific Fleet was at sea the 25 ocean-going submarines in position off the Hawaiian Islands would have a major role. If it was at anchor then five two-man miniature submarines, carried to their target on the backs of larger submarines, would slip past the American defenses and wait on the bottom of Pearl Harbor for the air attack to begin. They would then fire their torpedoes and attempt to escape. It was virtually a suicide mission.

The war-warning message received by Lieutenant-General Short on 27 November, the day after Nagumo's force left the Kuriles, included the instruction to conduct reconnaissance. To Short this was a puzzle. Ordinarily, long-range reconnaissance was an Army Air Force duty, but the Hawaiian District simply did not have the aircraft. The only planes Short had capable of flying the 300 miles out from Oahu were 12 elderly B-18 twin engined bombers and six B-17s (the other six having been cannibalized to keep them flying). On 21 March, Short had made the Hawaiian Joint Air Agreement with Rear Admiral Claude C Bloch, commander of the Fourteenth Naval District (Hawaii), stipulating that the Navy should take responsibility for long-range reconnaissance, and this had been approved both by the Army Chief of Staff, General George C Marshall, and by his opposite number, Admiral Harold R 'Betty' Stark, Chief of Naval Operations. Short therefore assumed that the reconnaissance instruction was general, aimed at other commanders – MacArthur in the Philippines, for example – and did nothing.

As if to underline the point, on the night of 6 December 12 B-17s of the 38th and 88th Reconnaissance Squadrons would fly from California to Hickam Field on Oahu. Stripped down and without machine guns to save weight for the 14-hour flight, they would land on Sunday morning virtually out of fuel. But they were not for Short's command. After refueling they were to fly on to Clark Field in the Philippines. As was normal practice, although supposedly secret, the US Army paid for KGMB Hawaiian radio to play music through the night when planes were flying to Oahu, in order to provide a radio fix, and this flight would be no exception.

Short's remaining aircraft were based at three airfields on Oahu: Hickam Field, Wheeler Field and Bellows Field, with satellite airstrips at Barber's Point and Haleiwa. In total the Army Air Force had available 99 Curtiss P-40 Kittyhawk fighters and 12 A-20 light bombers, together with 36 P-36 and 14 P-26 fighters and two A-12 light bombers, all obsolete types, plus a handful of utility aircraft. Of these only the Kittyhawks were of value for air defense, if they could be got airborne in time. There were six Army radar stations on Oahu, in operation daily except Sunday from 0700 to 1100 and except Saturday and Sunday from 1200 to 1600. Following the alert, Short ordered an extra daily radar watch, including weekends, from 0400 to 0700. Although not expecting an air attack, Short regarded this as good for training.

The warning message sent to Short specified that whatever action he took, 'these measures should be carried out so as not, repeat not, to alarm civil population or disclose intent.' He therefore opted for the lowest of his planned alerts, an anti-sabotage drill aimed principally at any Japanese subversives already on Oahu. Among other precautions, this involved keeping ammunition for all weapons, including anti-aircraft guns, locked securely some distance from the guns themselves, and parking aircraft wingtip-to-wingtip in the middle of their fields, without fuel or ammunition, making them easier to guard against intruders. This drill meant that, even if alerted by radar, it would take Short's fighters at least an hour to get airborne and into action.

Within hours of receiving his alert on 27 November, Short radioed Washington, 'Report department alerted to prevent sabotage. Liaison with Navy reurad four seven two twenty seventh'. If the War Department intended Short to go on full alert, the first part of his signal should have revealed that he had misunderstood his orders. The second part was a coded reference to the Joint Air Agreement which, again, should have reminded Washington that Short could not reconnoiter. In the confusion and pressure of the approach to war, both points

LEFT: The Japanese ocean going submarine *I-68*, one of the submarines deployed off the Hawaiian Islands as part of the Pearl Harbor plan.

BELOW: The USS *Enterprise* shortly before Pearl Harbor, being overflown by aircraft of its own VS-6 Squadron of Douglas SBD Dauntless dive bombers.

BELOW RIGHT: Vice-Admiral William F. 'Bull' Halsey, commander of the Pacific Fleet Carrier Force.

were missed. Short's emphasis on training, his fixation with security and sabotage, and his failure to be 'air minded,' were not unusual in the peacetime Army of his day, but together they combined with catastrophic effect for the defense of Pearl Harbor.

Admiral Kimmel's problem was no less difficult. Rear Admiral Bloch's scouting forces were simply inadequate for any kind of long-range reconnaissance. At the end of October 1941 the scouting strength of Fourteenth Naval District was 27 elderly PBY-3 Catalina amphibious aircraft. By 23 November, a further 54 new PBY-5 Catalinas had arrived, with the usual deficiencies in spares and equipment. One of these Catalina squadrons was based at Midway, and on 1 December Admiral Kimmel ordered a further squadron to Wake Island. This left a notional strength of 57 Catalinas at Ford Island and the satellite field of Kaneohe Point, of which about half could be put into the air at any one time. By this date, with the *Yorktown* gone and the *Saratoga* not yet returned to Pearl Harbor, Kimmel had only two carriers available, the *Enterprise* of only 19,800 tons, and the *Lexington*. The Catalinas, together with the reconnaissance aircraft from these carriers, were barely sufficient to cover the most important approach route, to the southwest of Oahu. Indeed, in the week following the 'war warning' of 27 November, crews and aircraft became so worn out that a

rest was ordered, and on the morning of Sunday 7 December just three PBY-5s were airborne. At no time did Bloch's search crews even attempt to reconnoiter northward.

If the two commanders on Oahu rated a Japanese air attack as unlikely, it can hardly be said that Washington rated it any higher. In the first week of November, Kimmel and Short had been asked to plan the reinforcement of Wake and Midway with up to a wing of P-40 fighters, about half of Short's effective fighter strength. On 26 November the two men agreed to send the lesser reinforcement of a squadron of Marine F-4F Wildcat fighters to Wake on board the *Enterprise*. With the existing state of tension, including a known threat from Japanese submarines, Vice-Admiral William F 'Bull' Halsey, commander of the Pacific Fleet carrier force, asked Kimmel for instructions. 'Goddammit,' Kimmel replied, 'use your common sense!' The aggressive Halsey took this as permission to go to war. On the morning of 28 November *Enterprise* left harbor together with three battleships and all their normal escorts as if for training. Once clear of the islands, the battleships group (Task Force 2) split off for routine exercizes, while the carrier group (Task Force 8) set off for Wake with orders from Halsey to engage any unidentified submarine or aircraft as hostile. After delivering its fighters to Wake, the *Enterprise* was scheduled to return to Pearl

A clear warning at this stage
would have put the Hawaiian Military District
on full alert.

Harbor at about 0700 hours on the morning of 7 December.

Despite the threat of war, Army, Navy and State Department Intelligence in Washington had no single clear view of what was going to happen. The Far Eastern Section of Army Intelligence (G-2) jumped the gun by predicting that the United States would be attacked on Sunday 30 November, while some Intelligence specialists offered 50-to-1 odds against a Japanese attack before March, and others in Naval Intelligence believed that, since Admiral Kimmel had received a war warning, the whole Pacific Fleet was at sea according to its war plan. Using radio traffic analysis, even when they could not break the Japanese codes, the Americans built up a reasonably clear picture of the first moves of the Southern Operation. They could not, however, tell whether the attack would come only against the British and Dutch, or would include the Philippines as well. On 1 December the Japanese suddenly changed all their call signs, over 15,000 different designations, throwing Commander Rochefort's codebreakers at Pearl Harbor into brief confusion. On 2 December Kimmel's Intelligence staff reported that although most of the Japanese forces were moving south they could not confirm the position of 1st or 2nd Carrier Divisions (5th Carrier Division was not even known to exist). Naval Intelligence in Washington showed the missing carriers as probably still in harbor in Japan.

Years later, a story would emerge of how First Air Fleet was tracked across the Pacific by two independent radio listening posts. One was the radio room of the commercial liner SS *Lurline* in the Pacific, which picked up on 1 December signals broadcast in clear with Japanese call signs, placed by direction finding firmly northwest of Hawaii. On docking at Honolulu on 3 December the *Lurline*'s radio men passed their suspicions to the FBI. At the same time, communications experts in the US Navy's Twelfth Naval District (San Francisco) detected strange radio signals that, again, were tracked to the North Pacific. The problem with these stories is that the First Air Fleet was not transmitting. It kept strick radio silence except for low-power signals between Nagumo on *Akagi* and the rest of his force. If these were being intercepted occasionally, it was not enough to convince Washington or Ohau that the missing carriers were steaming for Pearl Harbor.

On 3 December Admiral Yamamoto came to the Emperor's Palace in Tokyo and received the Imperial Rescript, his official authorization to go to war. This was no more than a formality, the initial moves of the Southern Operation having already begun a week beforehand. Later that day, Admiral Nagumo received the coded signal from Tokyo, 'Climb Mount Niitaka 1208,' confirming that hostilities would commence at midnight on 8 December, Tokyo time. In the early hours of 4 December came a message relayed from the consulate in Honolulu: the *Lexington*, and six battleships were inside Pearl Harbor (including by mistake USS *Utah*, an elderly battleship used as a target ship for training purposes). Later that morning Nagumo – going beyond his instructions – issued orders that any non-Japanese ships or aircraft encountered were to be attacked, disabled, and if necessary sunk.

Admiral Kimmel, meanwhile, was busy carrying out the directive of 27 November, which had ordered him to 'execute the appropriate defensive deployment preparatory to carrying out the tasks assigned' in the Navy's war plan. This included reinforcing Midway Island, and on Friday 5 December the *Lexington*, three heavy cruisers and five destroyers (Task Force 12) left Pearl Harbor for Midway. Later that day two more heavy cruisers left on a routine mission. Also on the afternoon of 5 December two destroyers picked up a mysterious underwater contact about five miles from Oahu, possibly a submarine. It was Friday, and until Monday morning the main Battle Fleet, seven battleships and their escorts under Vice-Admiral William Pye, would remain at anchor in Pearl Harbor, along with submarines, minesweepers, seaplane tenders, assorted auxiliaries and harbor craft, in total some 85 warships including Kimmel's own flagship, USS *Pennsylvania*, which was in drydock.

At dawn on 6 December, First Air Fleet completed its last refueling, its oilers with a single escorting destroyer broke away, and the warships plunged southward. A clear warning at this stage would have put the Hawaiian Military District on full alert, and sent the battle fleet to sea. Even an hour's notice would have been enough to equip the anti-aircraft guns, both on shore and onboard ship, to get the fighters up, and make ready the damage control parties. But even after President Roosevelt's remark, late on 6 December, that war was about to break out, there was no clear warning sent from Washington.

The situation was somehow impossible: that Japan was about to attack the United States seemed obvious, but it was also ridiculous. Instead, the American government waited. On Oahu, also, despite the war tension, senior officers attended dinner parties or went to bed early. Admiral Kimmel and Lieutenant-General Short had a golf game fixed for Sunday morning. Kimmel and his staff believed that, after 27 November, Short was on full alert. Short and his staff believed that Bloch's aircraft were carrying out their reconnaissance function as agreed. Since 1932 it had been known that Pearl Harbor was vulnerable to air attack, but for the Japanese to make such an attack seemed quite impossible.

Not that it really mattered, but the war had already started between Japan and Great Britain. At about midday on 7 December local time, a British Catalina flying out from Singapore sighted the Japanese invasion convoy bound for northern Malaya, and was shot down by Japanese Army fighters. The time in Oahu was 1830 hours on 6 December. At shortly after 0100 hours on 8 December the warships accompanying this convoy began to bombard the Malayan coast. Thanks to the time difference, there were still more than two hours to go before the attack on Pearl Harbor.

On Sunday morning in Washington the fourteenth and final part of the message to Ambassador Nomura had been received and broken by the Magic codebreakers. It was not a declaration of war, or even a breaking of diplomatic relations, but simply an announcement by the Japanese government that 'it is impossible to reach an agreement through further negotiations.' By 0900 hours, Magic had also broken the order from Tokyo to Nomura to present the full message to Secretary Hull at 1300 hours Washington time. It being a Sunday, it took precious minutes to find Admiral Stark and General Marshall. Stark considered contacting Kimmel directly, then changed his mind to consult Marshall. Both men then agreed on sending a warning to all American commands. It went out in code over Marshall's signature at noon, advising that the Japanese were presenting 'what amounts to an ultimatum' at 1300 hours. 'Just what significance the hour set may have we do not know,' the message ran, 'but be on alert accordingly.' It was still, perhaps, not too late.

The message reached most commands a few minutes later. But heavy atmospheric static blocked the Army's radio

ABOVE: The destroyer USS *Ward*, taken just after its launch in 1918, showing the irregular camouflage used in World War I.

RIGHT: A Japanese pilot prepares for the attack on Pearl Harbor.

communications with the Hawaiian Islands, and the only way to get this vital despatch through was through Western Union teletype to Honolulu. Sent at 1217 hours (0647 hours Hawaiian time), it would arrive, still encoded, by despatch rider at Short's headquarters about 15 minutes after the Japanese attack began.

Off Pearl Harbor, at about 0342 hours on 7 December, the minesweeper USS *Condor* relayed a periscope sighting to the destroyer USS *Ward*. The contact was reported, but not passed on. When the *Condor* returned to Pearl Harbor at 0500 hours it is probable that two of the Japanese miniature submarines followed it inside. Thirty minutes later, the two heavy cruisers with First Air Fleet, *Chickuma* and *Tone*, each launched a single Mitsubishi F1M2 'Pete' seaplane. Their job was to reconnoiter Pearl Harbor and Lahaina ahead of the first wave, to provide the latest possible information on the state of the defenses. At 0645 hours both planes appeared from the north on Oahu's radar. The radar station passed the information on to its central Information Center, where the only officer on duty was an inexperienced

ABOVE: Deck crew cheer as the first of the Japanese aircraft take off for Oahu.

LEFT: A Japanese deck officer watches the take-off, standing ready to record the returning aircraft on the board beside him.

ABOVE RIGHT: A Japanese newsreel shows the first Zeros ready to take-off.

lieutenant. The sighting was logged, and no more was thought of it. At 0550 hours the first wave of aircraft began to launch from the carriers, and by 0605 hours all but two of the fighters had taken off safely. At 0620 hours Commander Fuchida led them toward their target, homing in on KGMB radio which was still playing. With the first wave gone, the second wave began to take off at 0630 hours. The target was 90 minutes' flight time away.

Just as Nagumo's second wave was taking off, another of the Japanese miniature submarines attempted to slip past the supply ship USS *Antares* into Pearl Harbor. The *Antares* informed the destroyer *Ward*, which this time made no mistake, ramming the submarine at 0640 hours and following this up with a full depth-charge pattern. Again, not that it really mattered, but Japan and the United States were now at war, and the United States had fired the first shot. The Japanese strike was still more than an hour away when the *Ward* radioed through to Rear Admiral Bloch's head-quarters that it had sunk a hostile sub-marine. The officer on duty first phoned Admiral Kimmel, who was already up preparing for his golf game. Kimmel's

immediate reaction was that this might be a false alarm, and that he should wait for more information. Bloch, reached shortly after Kimmel, agreed. In fact, confirmation was about to come, since at 0706 hours the *Ward* sighted and sank a further miniature submarine trying to get into Pearl Harbor. No-one thought to inform the Army of either sinking, even as a matter of routine.

The Army, meanwhile, was making mistakes of its own. Just after 0700 hours Kahuku Point radar station picked up the lead elements of Fuchida's incoming airstrike, at least 50 aircraft coming in from almost due north. The immediate reaction of the two enlisted men on duty was that their equipment was broken. Once they were satisfied that it was not, they called the Informa-tion Center. There, the lieutenant on duty assumed that the radar had picked up the B-17s coming in from California, and again did nothing. It was already too late to make any difference to the Army, but the information that the attack was coming from the north would later have been crucial to the Navy, who were not informed.

At 0735 hours the seaplane from the *Chikuma*, circling over Pearl Harbor,

radioed 'Enemy formation at anchor: nine battleships, one heavy cruiser, six light cruisers are in the harbor.' The pilot had included the *Utah* and the drydocked *Pennsylvania* in the battleship total, and mistaken one light cruiser for heavy. At the same time, the seaplane from *Tone* reported Lahaina clear. Neither sea-plane could find the American carriers. The Japanese had already had more than their share of luck on Operation Hawaii, but now a small part swung the other way. The *Enterprise* had developed engine trouble and was still 200 miles west of Oahu, just within range for Hal-sey to fly off some of his aircraft back to Ford Island.

At 0740 hours the first wave of Japanese aircraft arrived unannounced and unexpected over Pearl Harbor, in the very heart of the American defenses. 'Below me lay the whole US Pacific Fleet in a formation I would not have dared to dream even in my most optimistic dreams,' Commander Fuchida later wrote, 'I have never seen ships, even in the deepest deep, anchored at a distance of 500-1000 yards from each other. A war fleet must be on the alert.' It was what Fuchida had hoped and planned for, but he could scarcely believe his eyes or his luck. 'Had these Americans never heard of Port Arthur?' He radioed back to the *Akagi* the agreed code for complete surprise – the Japanese word for 'Tiger' three times – *'Tora! Tora! Tora!'*

The reaction from the ground, and from the crews in 'Battleship Row' alongside Ford Island, was either that the Army Air Force was putting on a display or that some of its pilots had gone mad. Even for a few seconds after bombs and torpedoes began to drop from the Japanese planes, the truth refused to register. Not until 0758 hours was the radio message sent out *'Air Raid Pearl Harbor, This Is No Drill!'* Chance and quick reactions saved many lives, but nothing could save the ships at anchor. Fuchida's training had stressed that if surprise was achieved each pilot was to make several passes to make sure of his target, and for 10 minutes the sky was criss-crossed with turning aircraft.

The first successful hits probably came at about 0750 hours from torpedoes launched against the light cruiser *Raleigh* and the *Utah* beside it, a pointless target attacked by mistake in the excitement. The light cruiser *Helena* and the minelayer *Oglala* were both crippled by a single torpedo aimed at the nearby *Pennsylvania*. Torpedoes launched at Battleship Row struck the *Oklahoma*, the *West Virginia*, the support ship *Vestal* and, tied up alongside, the *Arizona*, which seemed to lift out of the water with the explosion.

Admiral Kimmel had been told by phone of the attack within minutes of it starting, and raced by car to the harbor. He arrived at about 0805 hours, just in time to see Vice-Admiral Pye's flagship, *California*, take a torpedo hit. Although counterflooding was holding most of the stricken ships on an even keel, a fourth torpedo hit was too much for the *Okla-*

BELOW: Pearl Harbor in the first 10 minutes of the attack, taken from one of the Japanese aircraft. Battleship Row is on the far side of Ford Island, where the plume of water shows a torpedo striking USS *West Virginia*, and the torpedo bomber can be seen turning away above the stricken battleship.

RIGHT: A view of Battleship Row from an overflying Japanese aircraft. Top to bottom: *Arizona* and *Vestal*, both hit, *Tennessee* and *West Virginia*, *Maryland* and *Oklahoma*, with the outboard ships also hit. Note the oil slicks from the holed battleships.

LEFT: Seen from the far shore, Japanese bombs fall around *Tennessee* and *West Virginia.*

RIGHT: One of the Japanese miniature submarines beached after the attack.

BELOW RIGHT: A US Army antiaircraft crew at Hickam Field, shown on exercise before the attack.

BELOW: Beneath the smoke pall, USS *Arizona* sinks as its forward magazine explodes.

*The second wave of Japanese aircraft
arrived over Pearl Harbor at 0900 hours
to face a determined defense.*

homa, which capsized and turned over. The tanker *Neosho* was hit and for a moment threatened to explode the fuel tanks on Ford Island, part of the harbor tank farm containing millions of gallons. *West Virginia* was hit twice more. *Tennessee* and *Maryland*, moored inboard of *West Virginia* and *Oklahoma*, received two bomb hits each. At this point some of Halsey's aircraft from the *Enterprise* arrived over Ford Island, and were fired at by anti-aircraft gunners in no mood for fine distinctions. Then the *Arizona* blew up with a bomb in its forward magazine, the bottom of its hull ripped out. As he watched, a spent bullet shattered the glass in front of Admiral Kimmel and bounced off his chest. Kimmel picked it up. 'It would have been merciful had it killed me,' he said.

Meanwhile, the Navy, Marines and Army Air Force aircraft on the ground were sitting targets for the Zeros and Vals, while ammunition was found for machine guns and anti-aircraft guns. Incredibly, four of the six airworthy B-17s managed to take off. Even more remarkably, while the raid was going on the 12 B-17s from California arrived over Hickam Field, into a swarm of Japanese fighters, and diverted to land all over Oahu. Every one of them got down safely. The Navy aircraft, particularly the Catalinas, were fighting to get into the air to search for the enemy carriers – the direction of which the Army already knew. But at 0810 hours Lieutenant-General Short had issued orders for his highest state of alert, defense against a full-scale invasion, and gone to his protected command bunker.

As the first wave of Fuchida's aircraft turned for home at 0820 hours, a handful of smaller ships were clearing the mouth of Pearl Harbor, led by the destroyer USS *Helm*. On its way, the destroyer engaged and probably disabled another of the Japanese miniature submarines. About half an hour separated the two Japanese attack waves, time to issue anti-aircraft ammunition, make repairs, get a few ships to sea and a few aircraft into the air. While this was going on another destroyer, USS *Monaghan*, spotted and attacked a miniature submarine in the harbor at 0839 hours. So far, none of the submarines had scored a successful kill.

The second wave of Japanese aircraft arrived over Pearl Harbor at 0900 hours to face a determined, if disorganized, American defense. Two P-40 pilots who had got airborne saved Haleiwa airfield from serious damage, but not enough American aircraft and anti-aircraft guns

ABOVE: The USS *Nevada* on fire.

RIGHT: Damage to the destroyer USS *Downes* in dry dock, hit by Japanese bombers aiming for the USS *Pennsylvania*.

LEFT: The wreckage of USS *Downes* and USS *Cassin* (on right) with the USS *Pennsylvania* behind them.

had survived to make much difference over Pearl Harbor. USS *Nevada* had got up steam and, with a gaping hole in its bows, attempted to clear the harbor, only to be crippled by further hits. In order to prevent the battleship sinking in mid-channel, it was beached close to the *Arizona* at 0907 hours. The *Pennsylvania* was hit once, and in trying for a second hit the Japanese wrecked the nearby destroyers *Shaw, Cassin* and *Downes*. The *Raleigh* and the *Helena* were both hit a second time, and another cruiser, the *Honolulu*, was also hit once.

At 0950 hours the destroyer *Blue* attacked a miniature submarine in the

harbor, and at 1004 hours the cruiser *St Louis* was clearing the anchorage when possibly the same submarine fired two torpedoes at it and missed. This was the only known submarine attack of the day. The *St Louis* believed that it sank the submarine in reply, accounting for all five including one which was forced to surface. Shortly after 1010 hours, as the order was given to abandon ship on the *Arizona* and on the capsizing mine-sweeper *Oglala*, the last of the Japanese aircraft departed.

Oklahoma and *Arizona* lay overturned and sunk beyond salvation. *California, Nevada* and *West Virginia* had sunk set-

tling upright in the shallow waters. *Maryland, Tennessee* and *Pennsylvania* were all damaged. *Utah*, three light cruisers, three destroyers and four auxiliary vessels had also been sunk or damaged. Of the American aircraft, 154 fighters, 52 bombers and nine reconnaissance planes had been wrecked, of which 117 were later written off. Ford Island, Hickam Field, Wheeler Field, Bellows Field, Kaneohe Point and Ewa Bay had all been severely damaged. The Navy had lost 2008 dead and 710 wounded, mostly from the *Arizona* and *Oklahoma.* The Marine Corps had lost 109 dead and 69 wounded, the Army, including the Air Force, 218 dead and 35 wounded. Civilian casualties were 68 dead and 35 wounded.

The aircraft from Fuchida's first wave started to return to First Air Fleet at about 1010 hours. The bombers were at once rearmed with torpedoes, in case the American carriers were in the area and

RIGHT: Fire boats attempting to control the fires on board the USS *West Virginia*.

*'By the time we've finished, the
Japanese language will be spoken only in Hell.'
(William 'Bull' Halsey.)*

ABOVE: Another view of the USS *Arizona* going down.

LEFT: The USS *Arizona* sinks.

chose to fight. By the time the last of the second wave returned at midday, Fuchida's Intelligence picture had *Pennsylvania*, *Oklahoma*, *West Virginia*, and *Tennessee* as all sunk, *Utah* (identified correctly), *Vestal*, *Oglala* and *Neosho* also sunk, *Arizona*, *Maryland*, and the destroyer *Shaw* seriously damaged, and *California* and *Nevada* moderately damaged. The enemy air strength had been massively depleted, and the Hawaiian Islands were wide open. Japanese losses had been five Kates, one Val and three Zeros from the first wave, 14 Vals and six Zeros from the second wave – 29 aircraft plus a further 74 damaged.

At this moment, First Air Fleet could have wrecked Oahu Island and Pearl Harbor Naval Base from end to end. But there was not enough time to convert the Kates from torpedoes to bombs, fly off another strike and recover it before dusk. Genda and Fuchida argued that Nagumo must instead maneuver southward, seek out and sink the American carriers, and go back to finish off Oahu in a day or so. For Nagumo the risk was too great. Over a quarter of his aircraft had been lost or damaged, there might be four unlocated American carriers nearby, and he had carried out his mission so far without loss to his carriers. As far as he was concerned, the objective had been achieved.

He ordered First Air Fleet to run west for safety, a decision confirmed by Admiral Yamamoto by radio next day.

In Washington, the Japanese embassy proved less efficient at decrypting and typing the long final message from Tokyo than the Magic codebreakers. The unfortunate Ambassador Nomura, who had no idea that the attack had taken place, was forced to ask for a delay in his meeting with Secretary Hull. The two men met at 1420 hours, by which time Hull knew all about Pearl Harbor. 'I have never seen a document that was more crowded with infamous falsehoods and distortions,' he told Nomura, 'on a scale so huge that I never imagined until today that any Government on the planet was capable of uttering them.' Nomura learned of Pearl Harbor when he returned to his embassy.

At Pearl Harbor itself, among the wreckage, Admiral Kimmel quietly disappeared into his office for a while. When he emerged, he had taken off the shoulder boards with the four stars of a full Admiral which went with his appointment as Commander-in-Chief, and replaced them with the two stars of his permanent rank of Rear Admiral. And on board the *Enterprise*, 'Bull' Halsey made a vow, 'By the time we've finished, the Japanese language will be spoken only in Hell.'

LEFT: The wreckage of a Japanese 'Val' dive bomber recovered by the Americans from Pearl Harbor after the raid. Note the 'tube' type of bombing sight in front of the cockpit.

ABOVE: The US Navy air base at Wheeler Field on fire after the Japanese attack. Note the rows of parked aircraft.

LEFT: The wreckage of a P-40 Kittyhawk beside a damaged hangar at Wheeler Field.

ABOVE RIGHT: One of the B-17s that arrived at the same time as the Japanese, hit on the ground after landing safely at Bellows Field.

RIGHT: Hickam Field under attack by the Japanese.

CHAPTER FIVE

THE RECKONING

ON THE day after Pearl Harbor, President Roosevelt went before Congress for the formality of a declaration of war against Japan. 'Yesterday, December 7, 1941,' he told them, 'a date which will live in infamy, the United States was suddenly and deliberately attacked.' So, by a choice of words, a brave and daring Japanese feat of arms was converted into a sneak attack, an act at once wicked and cowardly. The errors in Washington and Oahu that had made Pearl Harbor possible were swallowed in American righteous indignation, and hatred of Japan rapidly became a paranoid fear of Japanese Americans as dangerous subversives.

By June 1942 about 119,000 Hawaiian Japanese, Japanese immigrants to the United States and American citizens of Japanese origin living in California, Washington, Oregon and Arizona had been imprisoned without trial and their property confiscated. Some did not survive their time in the internment camps. Although many other Japanese Americans volunteered for the armed forces they were not considered trustworthy enough to fight against Japan. No such action, of course, was taken against Americans of German origin when, true to their promise before Pearl Harbor, the Germans declared war on the United States on 12 December. Not until 1989 did the United States government finally apologize for this gross violation of its own Constitution, and pay compensation to the surviving victims.

Even as President Roosevelt was speaking, the rest of the Southern Operation was going ahead. Despite the warning of Pearl Harbor, peacetime habits remained on the Allied side for a few days, and commanders seemed incapable of learning even the most elementary lessons of security and preparation. A few hours after Pearl Harbor, American forces at Clark Field in central Luzon,

PREVIOUS PAGES: The might of the US Navy – aircraft waiting to take off from the deck of an American carrier during the Battle of the Coral Sea.

RIGHT: President Roosevelt, wearing a black arm-band for the dead of Pearl Harbor, signs the Declaration of War against Japan on the day after the raid.

BELOW: Sailors of the US Navy laying Hawaiian garlands on the graves of comrades who died in the attack on Pearl Harbor.

LEFT: The drydocked USS *Pennsylvania*, showing only slight damage after the attack.

LEFT: Newspapers all over America published extra editions announcing the Japanese attack. For a time, war fever competed with Japanese spy scares.

RIGHT: US sailors in Chicago reading of the Japanese attack.

IT'S WAR!

Hostilities Declared by Japanese; 350 Reported Killed in Hawaii Raid

U.S. Battleships Hit; 7 Die in Honolulu

NEW YORK, Dec. 7. (A.P.)—Three hundred and fifty men were killed by a direct bomb hit on Hickam Field an N.B.C. observer reported tonight from Honolulu.

In addition to these casualties from an air raid by planes which the observer identified as Japanese, he said three United States ships, including the battleship Oklahoma, were attacked in Pearl Harbor.

Several of the attacking planes, which came from the south, were shot down, he said.

HONOLULU, Dec. 7. (A.P.)—Japanese bombs killed at least seven persons and injured many others, three seriously, in a surprise morning aerial attack on Honolulu today.

Army officials announced that two Japanese planes had been shot down in the Honolulu area.

The dead included three Caucasians, two Japanese and a 10-year-old Portuguese girl.

Several fires were started in the city area, but all were immediately controlled.

Governor Joseph B. Poindexter proclaimed M-Day emergency defense measures immediately in effect. He appointed Eduard Doty

LATE WAR BULLETINS

SHANGHAI, Dec. 8 (Monday.) (A.P.)—The Japanese have sunk the British gunboat Petrel as it lay off the International Settlement waterfront.

HONOLULU, Dec. 7. (U.P.) — Parachute troops were sighted off Pearl Harbor today.

TOKYO, Dec. 8 (Monday.) (A.P.)—An emergency session of the Japanese Cabinet was held at Premier Tojo's official residence at 7 a.m. today (2 p.m. Sunday, P.S.T.)

NEW YORK, Dec. 7. (U.P.)—The U.S.S. Oklahoma, a battleship, was set afire in today's air attack on Pearl Harbor, an N.B.C. broadcast from Honolulu said.

WASHINGTON, Dec. 7. (A.P.)—The Navy Department announced tonight that a censorship had been placed on all outgoing cablegrams and radio messages from the United States and its outlying possessions.

LONDON, Dec. 7. (UP)—The House of Commons was summoned tonight for a session tomorrow.

The House of Lords also was called.

An announcement from Prime Minister

Turn to Page 2, Column 2

Air Bombs Rained on Pacific Bases

WASHINGTON, Dec. 7. (A.P.)—The White House announced early tonight that the Navy had advised the President that Japan has attacked the island of Guam.

WASHINGTON, Dec. 7. (A.P.)—Japan declared war upon the United States today. An electrified nation immediately united for a terrific struggle ahead. President Roosevelt was expected to ask Congress for a declaration of war tomorrow.

During the day, Japanese planes bombed Manila, Honolulu, Pearl Harbor, and Hickam Field, Hawaii, without warning. In a broadcast from Honolulu, some 350 soldiers were reported dead at Hickam Field, with numerous casualties at the other points of attack. (The attack on Manila was announced by the White House. The Associated Press correspondent there reported at 1:25 p.m. (P.S.T.) that Manila was quiet.) President Roosevelt said he hoped the report of the bombing of the Philippine capital "at least is erroneous."

Then, the Tokyo government announced that Japan had entered a state of war with the United States and Great Britain a of 6 a.m., tomorrow (1 p.m. P.S.T. Sunday.)

But President Roosevelt hardly waited for the Japanese declaration. As soon as he heard of the bombing he ordered the Army and Navy to carry out previously prepared and highly secret plan for the defense of the country.

Army airmen engaged Japanese fighting planes over Honolulu In the city below them, the White House said, a heavy loss of life had been inflicted, together with extensive damage to property.

RIGHT: The front page of a special edition of the *Los Angeles Times*, 8 December 1941. In fact no formal declaration of hostilities was ever made by the Japanese — it was the United States that actually declared war.

RIGHT: President Roosevelt shakes hands with Lieutenant George S. Welch of the US Army Air Force, one of the P-40 pilots who managed to get airborne during the Japanese attack, shooting down four enemy aircraft.

the largest of the Philippines, were caught completely unprepared by a Japanese air raid and suffered heavy casualties. Two days later, on 10 December local time, the British battleship HMS *Prince of Wales* and the battle-cruiser HMS *Repulse*, returning to Singapore after a foray along the northern coast of Malaya without air cover or carrier support, were sunk by Japanese aircraft based in southern Indochina.

General MacArthur's notion that the Philippines could be defended was rapidly shown to be completely unrealistic when the Japanese launched their main invasion on 22 December. The resulting battle became the biggest disaster in American military history as unprepared Filipino troops proved incapable of standing against the Japanese. The last American and Filipino stronghold on the Philippines at Corregidor surrendered on 6 May 1942, after MacArthur had been ordered to safety. Guam fell on 10 December and Wake on 23 December. Meanwhile, the Japanese had snapped up Hong Kong on Christmas Day, and were advancing

Even as the smoke rose over the fleet at Pearl Harbor, it was obvious that the Japanese had lost the war.

LEFT: The British battleship HMS *Prince of Wales* sinking off the Malayan coast.

BELOW LEFT: The USS *Utah* in Pearl Harbor after the Japanese attack, being held upright by pontoons.

BELOW: American troops as prisoners of the Japanese following the surrender of the Philippines.

down the Malayan peninsula. Singapore surrendered on 15 February 1942, only five days after the main Japanese assault began, making its loss in turn the biggest disaster in British military history.

By the end of May 1942, virtually according to Japanese expectations, their defensive perimeter ran from China through Burma, down through the Andaman Islands, south of Sumatra, Java and Timor, coming north to take in the northern coast of New Guinea, then south again to include the Bismarck Islands, the Solomon Islands, and sharp north across the Pacific to the Gilberts, the Marshalls and Wake. The mountainous jungle of New Guinea held no natural resources vital to the Japanese, but their failure to secure it as part of their perimeter would create problems later. Otherwise, the Southern Opera-

tion had been a magnificent success for the Japanese Imperial Army and Navy. Not only was the Line of the Rising Sun in place, but the Japanese had pushed the British out of the Far East completely and into the Indian Ocean, threatening India and even the east coast of Africa with their warships.

Yet, even as the smoke rose over the crippled Pacific Fleet at Pearl Harbor, it was obvious to the Allied leaders that Japan had lost the war. On getting his declaration of war from Congress, Roosevelt cabled Winston Churchill, 'Today all of us are in the same boat with you and the people of the Empire and it is a ship which will not and cannot be sunk.' No-one understood this better than Churchill. Japan had committed itself to a hopeless war with the United States, the world's greatest industrial giant, and

LEFT: The British commander at Singapore, Lieutenant-General Percival, surrenders to the Japanese.

BELOW: British Prime Minister Winston Churchill addressing a special joint session of the United States Congress, three weeks after Pearl Harbor.

with the British Empire, the largest controller of natural resources and shipping in the world. 'Now at this very moment,' he later wrote, 'I knew the United States was in the war, up to the neck and in to the death. So we had won after all!'

At their first planning conference as full Allies, in Washington three weeks after Pearl Harbor, the British and Americans agreed that their basic strategy would remain the defeat of Germany and Italy first. Japan was defeated almost as an afterthought, crushed beneath the industrial and economic might of a United States which, almost until the very end, was making its main military effort elsewhere. The Japanese prediction, that after two years of war their position would be virtually hopeless, turned out to be remarkably accurate. The American involvement in the war against Japan, and with the Soviet Union in the war against Germany, meant that from December 1941, as Churchill put it, 'All the rest was merely the proper application of overwhelming force.'

It was the shock of Pearl Harbor, perhaps more than anything else, which absolutely guaranteed the Japanese defeat. Their attack on the Philippines would certainly have brought the United States into the war, but there was no romance to the Philippines for the American public. It was the destruction of beautiful and peaceful Oahu on a Sunday morning which gave the United States a determination and commitment to the war that might otherwise not always have been there. As Yamamoto knew, it was never very likely that American nerve would break in their war with Japan. Pearl Harbor removed the last possible doubt. It gave the average American the most tempting of opponents, a cowardly bully who attacked when your back was turned. And it gave the US Navy, of which Vice-Admiral Halsey was a fair representative, the most simple of motives for fighting the Japanese – revenge.

So, the main Japanese hope for winning the war – that the United States might lose heart – was undermined on its very first day by the attack at Pearl Harbor. Japan's fate was decided before the first shot had even been fired. It is therefore reasonable to ask the simple, obvious question – should the attack have taken place as it did?

The first point to make is that the American moralizing stance after 1919 on the threat of war, which so annoyed the Japanese, was of course entirely correct. Twentieth century all-out industrialized war is so destructive, so barbaric in its execution, that any nation which decides to pursue a policy which it believes may end in a major war commits a moral crime against humanity. This is exactly what the Japanese government decided on 2 July 1941. The Japanese may be excused for not knowing the nature of total war in 1919. The same excuse cannot be made in 1941, after four years' experience of war in China and two of observing the war in Europe. Yamamoto, Nagumo, Genda and Fuchida were great warriors born out of time, into a world that had become too dangerous for war. That to go to war with the United States was the one chance the Japanese saw for establishing themselves as a major power in Asia, or avoiding defeat in China, is irrelevant. That the Japanese regarded themselves as racially and culturally superior to the rest of the human race is an explanation for their behavior, but not an excuse. World War II, on all fronts, cost 57 million people dead, including over two million Japanese. For this, every Japanese involved in the Pearl Harbor plan must take part of the responsibility. Admiral Yamamoto, from his writings, seems always to have known that this was true.

The Imperial Rescript issued to Yamamoto on 3 December blamed Britain and the United States for the war. 'These two powers,' it ran, 'have increased military preparations on all sides of our Empire to challenge us. They have obstructed by every means our peaceful commerce and finally have resorted to a direct severance of economic relations thereby gravely menacing the existence of our Empire.' For the Japanese the conclusion was inescapable. 'This trend of affairs would, if left unchecked, endanger the very existence of our nation.' Every word of this was true. So, did the United States, either accidentally or deliberately, push Japan into war?

Economic sanctions were the invention of the League of Nations in the 1920s, and were seen not as a threat of war, but as an alternative action to the use of armed force. Since that time, although indirect sanctions over a period of years may produce some observable result, there has not been a single case of direct sanctions working anywhere in the world – that is, of a country retreating from a given major policy or territory as the direct result of overt economic pressure. The country under threat will either find an alternative economic source, or it will threaten to lash out with military action. This was not perhaps as well understood in 1941 as it is now. All the same, the United States government's decision to freeze Japanese assets on 26 July and impose an oil embargo on 1 August 1941 seems an appalling risk.

If it was the Japanese who chose war, it was the Americans who forced them to chose between war and the surrender of all their ambitions, the most humiliating political defeat in their country's history. For placing a dangerous enemy in this position, without fully appreciating the threat which this implied to the United States, President Roosevelt and his cabinet are open to severe criticism.

Once it was accepted that Japan needed the natural resources of the Far East in order to win its war with China, then the decision to go to war with the United States could not be faulted. In theory the Japanese could have left the Philippines unscathed in the middle of their Greater Asia Co-Prosperity Sphere. In practice, given the American reaction to their peaceful occupation of Indochina, they could hardly expect to occupy Malaya, Thailand and Borneo by force without the United States taking military action. Even if the Japanese government had believed this possible, their Army or Navy would certainly have forced the issue by attacking American ships or planes in the area.

On the other side, only the fondest of isolationists imagined that the United States could keep out of World War II forever. No government which pursued the blatantly pro-British, anti-German and anti-Japanese policies of the United States between 1939 and 1941 could in fairness be described as neutral. It is sometimes argued that the war with Japan was avoidable or unnecessary. But the idea that a sudden diplomatic breakthrough at the eleventh hour could have prevented war is, at best, fanciful. Japan and the United States had been on a collision course since the fall of France in June 1940, and only a complete reversal by one or the other could have prevented war.

It is also important to remember that the Southern Operation, a joint Army-Navy affair of great complexity taking months to plan, had been set fully in motion during the last week of November 1941. If, say, First Air Fleet had been somehow detected in the North Pacific on 1 December then the attack on Pearl Harbor would have been canceled, but the war would still have begun seven days later. Even if the whole Southern

*The Japanese could have helped their
war effort more if they had attacked the harbor, the
docks and the fuel dumps.*

Operation had been publicly 'blown' by the Americans it might still have gone ahead without surprise. If the Japanese had suddenly canceled everything – and it is hard to see how this was possible – then the underlying reasons for going to war in the first place would still remain. Indeed, so powerful was the American embargo that both the Japanese Army and Navy argued that they could not wait even a further six months for war. And beyond the issue of sanctions, like a giant sword hanging over Japan, was the Two-Ocean Navy and the shift of American industrial production to a war economy. In six months the problem of reconnaissance aircraft at Oahu, to name only one American deficiency, would have been more than solved.

Once war with the United States was decided, was Yamamoto correct to insist on Pearl Harbor as part of the operation? Here, the answer is only apparent with perfect hindsight. Yamamoto's target was not Pearl Harbor but the Pacific Fleet, which he needed out of action for six months while the Southern Operation was completed. But the American warplan, Rainbow Five, did not envisage an attack on the Japanese by the Pacific Battle Fleet for at least six months after the war had begun. Its role was defensive, not aggressive. In the event, after Pearl Harbor the Americans were forced to rely entirely on the fast carrier groups and submarines that had, in any case, been the basis of their Pacific strategy since the spring of 1941. The degree of US Navy interference in the Southern Operation was about the same as it would have been if Pearl Harbor had never taken place.

Even if the United States had suddenly changed its strategy, the battleships of the Pacific Battle Fleet were not the most modern type, and they did not have the support ships and oilers to reach far into the Pacific. It seems clear that the Japanese did not know this. Despite the myth of a network of Japanese spies on the Hawaiian Islands, virtually all Japanese Intelligence on the Pacific Fleet came from one or two Imperial Navy officers inside the Honolulu consulate. They could count the American ships and identify the type, but not much more. With hindsight, the Japanese decision to make the Pacific Fleet a target was a mistake. The Navy Staff, and even Yamamoto despite his 'air mindedness,' were too much disciples of Captain Mahan, believers in the *Kantai Kessen*, the clash of battleships, to realize that, for a while at least, these monsters posed

no threat to Japan.

Looked at in cold blood, therefore, the United States could afford to lose its Pacific Battle Fleet without really affecting its strategy. This fact has led to the most interesting, and the most terrible, of all the stories about Pearl Harbor: that not only did President Roosevelt and his government push Japan into war, but that Roosevelt knew the attack on Pearl Harbor would take place, and allowed it to happen in order to gain American popular support for the war. For obvious reasons, the evidence that has been produced to support this theory is very slight, and open to several different interpretations. But more importantly, for all the reasons given above, Roosevelt had absolutely no need to do anything of the kind. If, as his critics claim, he wanted war, then war was obviously coming. If he had known that Oahu or the Pacific Fleet were going to be attacked on the morning of Sunday 7 December then he and his commanders would have lost absolutely nothing by issuing a clear and unambiguous warning. That Pearl Harbor was caught by surprise is the single greatest proof that Washington, also, did not know what would happen.

Strictly speaking, this is because not even Admiral Nagumo knew until the early hours of 7 December precisely what he would do. If the Pacific Fleet had been at sea then his carriers would not have attacked Oahu at all, except possibly the air bases to limit interference from American fighters. It is important to remember that Nagumo's Kates took off with torpedoes and 800 kilogram anti-warship bombs, useless for attacking shore installations, before they had definite news of the Pacific Fleet's location, and rearmed with the same weapons after the Pearl Harbor strike. Indeed, to have done anything else with American carriers loose in the area would have been irresponsible – the battle for naval supremacy had to come before any attack on Oahu itself.

Nevertheless, the Japanese could have helped their war effort far more by attacking not the battleships in Pearl Harbor but the harbor installations, docks and workshops, above all the unprotected fuel, nearly 200 million US gallons (625,000 metric tons) in the tank farms on Ford Island and around Pearl Harbor. If these had been exploded, the resulting blast and fire would have caused far greater damage to the Pacific Fleet than was actually achieved. More importantly, Pearl Harbor was the only

ABOVE: The USS *Lexington* under attack during the Battle of the Coral Sea. Note the Japanese 'Kate' torpedo bomber making an attack run, visible just in front of the *Lexington*'s bow.

US Navy base in the Pacific west of California. If it could be wrecked to the point that it could no longer take capital ships, then the Americans would have to begin their return to the Pacific from 2000 miles farther back.

This line of argument suggests that Commanders Genda and Fuchida were right in asking Nagumo to hunt down the American carriers after the Pearl Harbor strike, and then return to devastate Oahu. This is much more obvious with hindsight, knowing that the only two American carriers in the area, *Lexington* and *Enterprise*, lay separated west of Oahu, with the Japanese between them and safety. Despite his losses at Pearl Harbor, Nagumo easily outnumbered the American carriers in aircraft. Almost as importantly, at this date all types of Japanese carrier aircraft decisively outranged their American counterparts. So far the US Navy had no idea of First Air Fleet's position, and if Nagumo had found the American carriers first he could have sunk both almost without risk to his own forces.

Perhaps, as a compromise, Nagumo might have pulled away north, and then returned to repeat his attack two days later, hoping to find *Enterprise* and *Lexington* back in harbor. Against that, the whole Southern Operation ran on a shoestring, and Nagumo could not easily afford the loss of even one carrier. In fact, *Soryu* and *Hiryu* were needed on their return home to support a second Japanese attack on Wake on 21 December after the first had failed. This suggests that, again, the Mahan fixation of most naval officers interfered with the logic of Japanese strategy. Nagumo's orders should have included the destruction of Pearl Harbor itself as well as the Pacific Fleet.

LEFT: American sailors abandon the sinking USS *Lexington* during the Battle of the Coral Sea.

If it had been possible, the best Japanese strategy would have been that most feared by Lieutenant-General Short. an invasion and occupation of the Hawaiian Islands by a Japanese amphibious task force. Commander Genda, in the early stages of his planning, did investigate this possibility. With Pearl Harbor under Japanese control, and the Imperial Navy's carriers and submarines free to roam the eastern Pacific, the United States would have faced a very difficult task indeed for the first year or more of the war. As a bonus, in the unlikely but not impossible event of the Pearl Harbor fuel stocks being taken intact, they could have kept the entire Imperial Navy supplied for nearly two months.

Against this, even if the Pacific Fleet could be overcome, to take and hold the Hawaiian Islands against Short's defenses would have required at least two Japanese infantry divisions supported by battleships. Clearly, these were not going to be available if the rest of the Southern Operation was to go ahead as planned, especially as the Navy Staff persisted in regarding Yamamoto's

plan with deep suspicion. Also, if it failed to achieve surprise, such a plan might have been fatal to the Japanese. It was while attempting an invasion of Midway Island supported by carriers on 4 June 1942 that the Japanese lost *Akagi, Kaga, Hiryu* and *Soryu* all together to three American carriers they did not know were in the area. The argument comes full circle to the central Japanese problem – attempting too much with too few resources.

This paradox at the heart of the Japanese planning is also at the heart of the fatal American hesitation in the last days and hours before the attack. Intelligence work is hardly an exact science, and the cultural and internal political factors surrounding the behavior of the Japanese government and armed forces in 1941 made them harder to predict than most. In the United States, as in many other countries, analysts were – and still are – taught to 'judge by capabilities, not intentions,' by what the enemy has the capacity to do, rather than what he might want to do. For almost all Americans in December 1941, the absolute bottom line was that Japan did not

BELOW: The Japanese carrier *Shoho* sinking from a torpedo hit during the Battle of the Coral Sea.

RIGHT: The Japanese carrier *Hiryu* takes evasive action to avoid bombs from B-17 high altitude bombers flown from Midway Island during the Battle of Midway. The B-17 proved less effective against warships than had been expected before the war. The *Hiryu* was sunk by American carrier aircraft later in the battle.

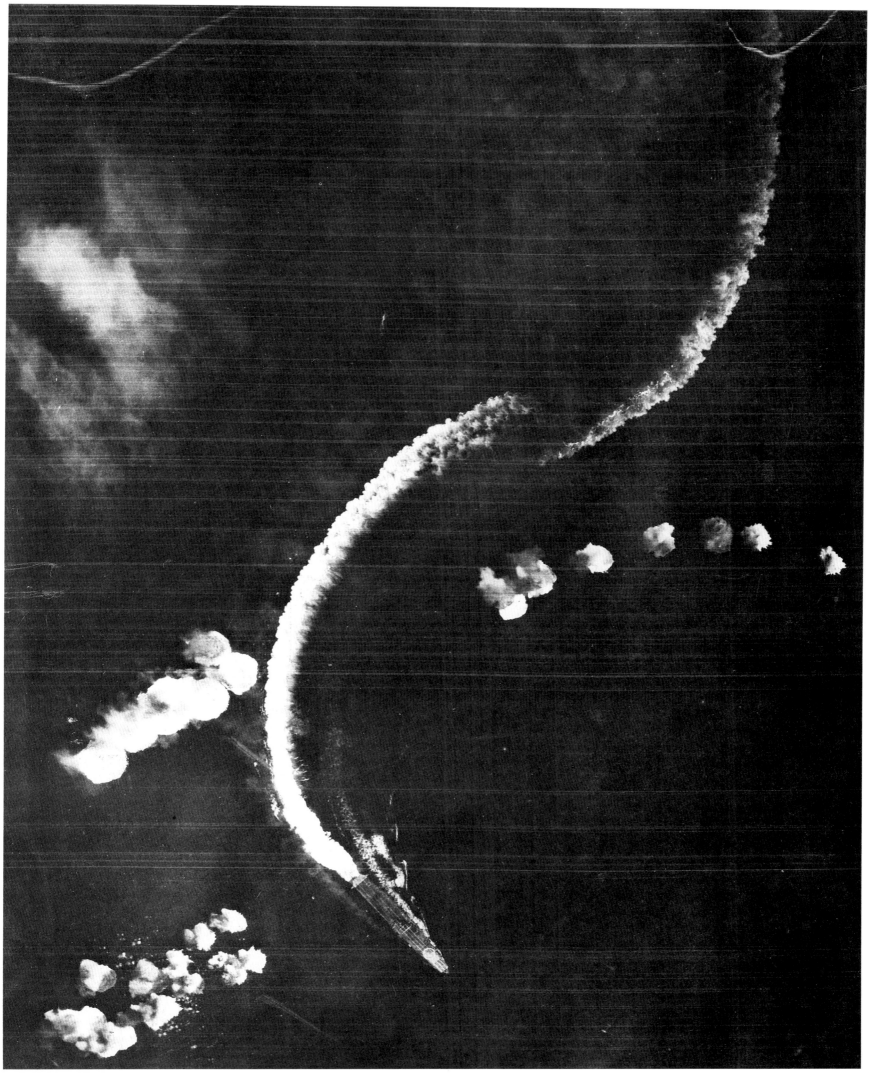

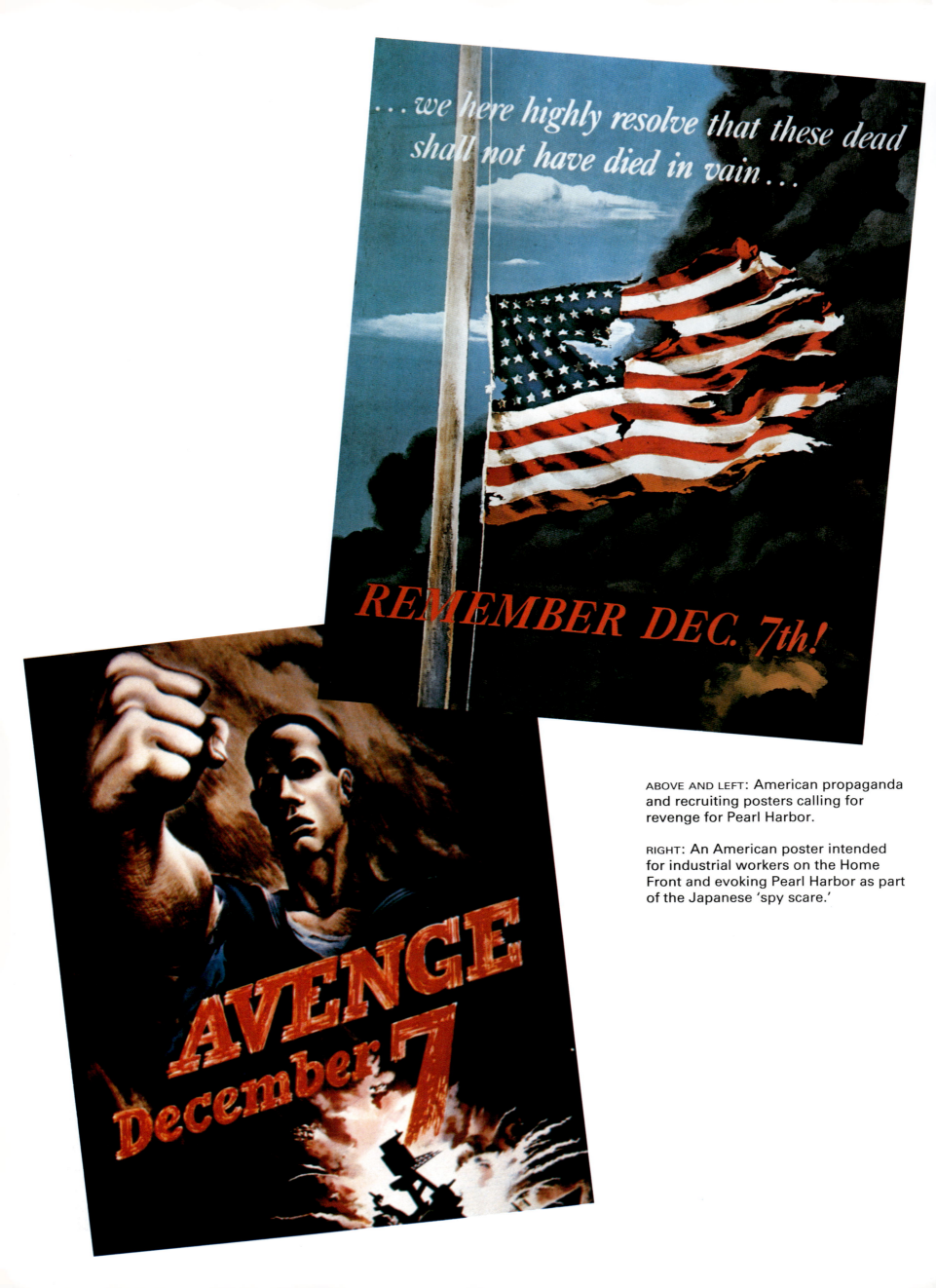

...we here highly resolve that these dead shall not have died in vain...

REMEMBER DEC. 7th!

AVENGE December 7

ABOVE AND LEFT: American propaganda and recruiting posters calling for revenge for Pearl Harbor.

RIGHT: An American poster intended for industrial workers on the Home Front and evoking Pearl Harbor as part of the Japanese 'spy scare.'

*The lasting legacy of the attack on
Pearl Harbor was the creation of the
Central Intelligence Agency on 18 September 1947.*

LEFT: The carrier USS *Yorktown* under Japanese attack during the Battle of Midway.

BELOW LEFT: The Japanese carrier *Hiryu* on fire and sinking during the Battle of Midway.

BELOW: USS *Yorktown*, also on fire and sinking during the Battle of Midway.

have the capability to make war against the United States. If there was a war then Japan would lose it, a fact as obvious to the Japanese as to the Americans. Therefore, by American reasoning, Japan would not attack and there could be no war.

As Secretary of the Navy James V Forrestal noted in one of the many reports and investigations into Pearl Harbor, 'although the imminence of hostile action by the Japanese was known, and the capabilities of the Japanese Fleet and Air Arm were recognized,' still, 'these factors did not reach the state of conviction in the minds of the responsible officers' to an extent 'sufficient to impel them to bring about the implementation of the plans that were necessary.' In other words, they could not bring themselves to believe in a Japanese attack. If, by some miracle of Intelligence work, a complete copy of Yamamoto's plans had arrived on President Roosevelt's desk on the day before Pearl Harbor, events would still have probably unfolded much as they did. Indeed, there were cases throughout World War II of commanders failing to react to captured enemy plans in exactly this manner. This failure of belief, together with the slow reactions of American officers familiar only with peacetime routine, and a very large slice of Japanese luck, is suffi-

cient explanation of how surprise was achieved.

Between December 1941 and July 1946 the United States undertook no fewer than eight official investigations into its own conduct over Pearl Harbor. Since, within days of the event, President Roosevelt's government had begun to protect itself by claiming that the blame for Pearl Harbor lay in Oahu and not in Washington, all these investigations came inevitably to have political overtones. One general conclusion, however, was that the American Intelligence failure was largely institutional, rather than the fault of individuals. The Army and the Navy seemed barely to have communicated with each other beyond the minimum requirements of orders. Crucial political Intelligence was denied the Navy on the grounds that it had no political role. The value of Magic was greatly reduced by its tiny circulation. Too many departments held individual pieces of the puzzle, no-one was in a position to put them all together and act on them. Following the last of the official investigations Congress determined that this should not happen again. The lasting legacy of Pearl Harbor was the creation, by the National Security Act of 18 September 1947, of the Central Intelligence Agency.

Although normally thought of as a

'spy' organization, the principal mission of the CIA is to prevent a second Pearl Harbor, by providing the United States government with advance warning of any impending enemy surprise attack on itself or its allies. In this it has been less than a complete success, failing to predict such surprise attacks as the North Korean, and later Chinese, invasion of South Korea of 1950, the Cuban Missile Crisis of 1962, the North Vietnamese 'Tet' Offensive of 1968, the Egyptian and Syrian attack on Israel of 1973 and the Iraqi attack on Kuwait of 1990. This makes the obvious point that surprise attacks such as Pearl Harbor are easier to explain with hindsight than they are to predict. Also, the institutional solution may not always be the correct one.

Admiral Kimmel and Lieutenant-General Short were relieved of their commands simultaneously on 16 December 1941, together with Short's Army Air Force commander. Neither man received

another command. Kimmel pressed hard but unsuccessfully for a court martial to clear his name, and until his death in 1968 continued to protest that he had been made a scapegoat. Short maintained a dignified silence until his death in 1949. Their defenders like to contrast their treatment with that given to General MacArthur. Despite his mistaken insistence that the Philippines could be held, which distorted American strategy, weakened Pearl Harbor's air defenses, and finally produced an unparalleled military disaster, MacArthur was rewarded by Roosevelt with the Medal of Honor, and promoted to become Supreme Allied Commander of the Southwest Pacific Theater in the war against Japan.

For a peacetime commander who saw training as his most important duty, Admiral Kimmel's behavior could hardly be faulted. Despite later claims, his orders of 27 November were only a

BELOW: The Japanese heavy cruiser *Mikuma*, hit by aircraft from the USS *Enterprise* during the Battle of Midway, on fire, abandoned and sinking.

BELOW RIGHT: A sinking Japanese patrol boat, seen through the periscope of the submarine USS *Seawolf*, April 1943. The *Seawolf* was one of the most successful American submarines of the war.

'war warning,' not instructions to go to war. It was Kimmel's good luck that carrying out those orders meant that neither of his carriers was in Pearl Harbor when the Japanese struck. Much of the rest was bad luck. The one threat he knew about and understood was from the Japanese submarines, and his command dealt with that superbly. His reaction on the morning of 7 December in waiting for confirmation of the submarine attack was not that of a wartime officer, who would have put the Pacific Fleet on alert without waiting. Nor would a wartime admiral have bunched his ships in the manner that so astonished Commander Fuchida. But those were lessons still to be learned.

Otherwise, what exactly had Kimmel done wrong? Most of the Pacific Fleet was at sea for training during the week. If he had kept it at sea over the weekend, it still needed to refuel and to anchor somewhere. Quite possibly Vice-Admiral Pye

might have chosen Lahina Roads, which in the event would have produced a worse disaster. For the rest, the air reconnaissance situation for the Hawaiian Islands was of course absurd, but it was improving. The underlying problem was the delay in United States rearmament until July 1940 – something which the isolationists who were so critical of President Roosevelt would themselves, of course, have delayed even further. Kimmel could have repeated his requests for more aircraft, but until they came off the production lines there was no point, particularly as the Atlantic and then MacArthur took priority. Under these circumstances a good peacetime officer learns not to annoy his superiors by asking for the moon.

Lieutenant-General Short was perhaps more to blame, particularly for the lack of air cover, and for refusing to consider the defense of the Pacific Fleet as part of his responsibility. His staff seems

to have made no effort even to enquire whether the Navy was carrying out its reconnaissance function as agreed, when an offer to help and a pooling of resources might have made at least a small improvement. But, if it would have been useful, long-range reconnaissance was not essential to the defense of Pearl Harbor. In 1940, the Royal Air Force had shown in the Battle of Britain how to link radar cover with fighters to provide a defense in a matter of minutes. Although Short had created the apparatus of such a system, he did not put it into practice. An aircraft is only of combat value when it is flying, and not even Short's extreme obsession with sabotage can excuse his emasculation of his own air defenses on 7 December.

Given that surprise was so total, that so much sheer luck went their way, it is remarkable how little damage the Japanese in fact caused to the Pacific Fleet. Partly due to Mahan's teachings,

partly from Japanese pride, the pilots concentrated on the American battleships at the expense of nearly every other ship in Pearl Harbor. Even so, of the five battleships sunk only *Arizona* and *Oklahoma* (together with *Utah*) were gone for good. *California, Nevada* and *West Virginia* were all eventually refloated, and took part in the assault on Okinawa in April 1945. Otherwise, only three out of nine light cruisers were damaged and a further three out of 67 destroyers. Not one of the 56 American submarines operating in the Pacific had been touched. Only 15 out of 85 warships inside the harbor had been attacked and hit. (As a curiosity, the cruiser *Phoenix*, hit by Japanese bomb fragments, was not sunk until 1982, when as the Argentine Navy's *General Belgrano* it fell victim to a British submarine during the Falklands War.) On the debit side, the Japanese had lost eight percent of their attacking aircraft, and suffered a further 21 percent damaged. Even despite the complete surprise, the battle was not as one-sided as it had been made to feel.

The Japanese submarine assault had been a fiasco. The miniature submarines took 100 percent losses without, as far as is known, hitting a single target. In open waters, none of the ocean-going submarines found any American ships. Although the Imperial Navy's Air Arm received a massive boost in prestige from

Pearl Harbor, the submarine service went into decline, receiving ever fewer of Japan's slender resources. With the United States it was the other way around, as the big ocean-going submarines played an ever increasing part in the economic blockade of Japan. On one patrol in August 1942 a single submarine, USS *Growler*, accounted for over 15,000 tons of merchant shipping, and in total American submarines sank 4,889,000 tons of Japanese merchant shipping in the course of the war.

Obviously, Pearl Harbor confirmed beyond all doubt the effectiveness of the aircraft carrier. The Battle of the Coral Sea, five months later, was the first major naval action in history in which two fleets engaged without ever setting sight on one another, fighting entirely with aircraft. In the course of the war the carrier operating in a fast attack group replaced the battleship as the capital ship of the world's navies. Even the Japanese giant battleship *Yamato*, launched in 1940, was finally sunk by American carrier aircraft off Okinawa on 7 April 1945. The second battleship of the class *Musashi*, was also lost to Vice-Admiral Halsey's carriers at the Battle of the Sibuyan Sea on 24 October 1944. The third and last, *Shinano*, was converted to the world's largest aircraft carrier at 72,000 tons. Launched in October 1944, it was sunk by the American sub-

ABOVE: The last act of Japanese desperation. A *kamikaze* suicide plane crashes into the deck of the battleship USS *New Mexico* off Okinawa, May 1945.

LEFT: The magazines of the Japanese flagship *Yamato* explode as it sinks off Okinawa. The three nearby destroyers give an idea of the battleship's size.

ABOVE, FAR LEFT: The last surviving carrier of First Air Fleet, the *Zuikaku*, under attack from American carrier planes during the Second Battle of the Philippine Sea, October 1944.

RIGHT: The American air base at Yontan on Okinawa in July 1945, following the successful capture of the island. P-51 Mustang fighters with drop tanks enabling them to reach Japan overfly a landing strip on which PBY-4 Catalinas are parked. By this date American domination of the air over Japan, and of the seas around it, was total.

marine *Archerfish* on 29 November without ever seeing action.

This did not mean that battleships were obsolete. In bad weather that prevented flying, and for delivering concentrated fire in support of amphibious landings, they still had a useful role to play. But the idea of the battle line, a fleet action of battleships deciding naval supremacy, was dead. Still, the old fight between the land-based bomber and the battleship was not resolved entirely in Billy Mitchell's favor. Although there were some successes, heavy bombers used from high altitude proved generally to be too inaccurate to attack warships. The B-17 Flying Fortress instead found its true role over Germany as a strategic area daylight bomber attacking factories and towns.

LEFT: The Japanese surrender on board USS *Missouri* in Tokyo Bay.

It was therefore an act of deliberate symbolism that when the Japanese armed forces surrendered unconditionally to the Allies on 15 August 1945, the surrender was formally accepted on 2 September 1945 by General of the Army Douglas MacArthur, on board not an aircraft carrier but a battleship, USS *Missouri*, in Tokyo harbor. Vice-Admiral Nagumo was not there. When the land forces under his command at Saipan were overwhelmed in June 1944, in the decisive American breakthrough of the Line of the Rising Sun, he had committed ritual suicide by way of apology to the Emperor. Admiral Yamamoto, also, was dead. A codebreak had given the Americans his flying schedule after the attack on Guadalcanal, and his personal aircraft was shot down over the jungle by 10 American P-38 fighters on 18 April 1943. Neither lived to see what both, with a Japanese sense of *karma*, might have easily predicted. Once more, unwanted and uninvited, American warships rode at anchor in Tokyo Bay.

ACKNOWLEDGMENTS

The author and publishers would
like to thank Ron Callow for
designing this book, Maria
Costantino for the picture research
and Ron Watson for compiling the
index. The following individuals and
agencies provided photographic
material:

Archiv Gerstenberg, pages: 12, 12-
13(all 3), 18(bottom), 19(bottom),
21(top).
Brompton Books, pages: 10(top),
11(bottom), 31(right), 34(top),
39(bottom), 40, 42, 44, 46(top &
bottom), 49, 55(top), 63, 64(top),
72, 73, 77(bottom), 82, 85(top).
Hoover Institute, pages:
25(bottom).
**Imperial War Museum, London,
pages:** 1, 21(center & bottom),
27(bottom), 30, 34(bottom), 38,
70-71, 76(top), 88(top), 90(both).
**Peter Newark's Military Pictures,
pages:** 2-3, 7(all 3), 8-9,
10(bottom), 11(top left & right), 14-
15(all 3), 16(bottom), 17(top),
18(top), 20(top), 31(left), 32, 33,
35(both), 43, 51(bottom), 57(right),
80, 81, 85(bottom), 98-99(all 3).
Robert Hunt Library, pages:
46(center above), 47(both), 51(top),
54, 65.
US Air Force, pages: 28(top),
76(bottom), 77(top), 86-87, 97, 106-
107.
US Department of Defense, pages:
108-109.
US Library of Congress, pages:
22-23, 45, 65(bottom), 84.
US National Archives, pages: 4-5,
16(top), 17(bottom), 27(top), 36-37,
50, 55(center), 57(left), 60(both),
61, 64(bottom), 66, 74-75, 78-79,
93, 96, 101, 102, 103, 105(both).
**US Naval Historical Center,
pages:** 24, 25(top), 28(bottom),
29(both), 39(top), 41, 46(center
bottom), 48, 52-53, 55(bottom), 56,
59(top), 62, 67(bottom), 68-69,
88(bottom), 89, 94, 100(both), 104.
US Naval Institute, page:
59(bottom).